Seeds
of
Grace

Sister Molly Monahan

Riverhead Books

a member of Penguin Putnam Inc.

New York

2001

Seeds
of
Grace

A Nun's Reflections
on the Spirituality
of Alcoholics
Anonymous

Certain names and identifying characteristics of individuals por-
trayed in this book have been changed to protect their privacy.

Riverhead Books
a member of
Penguin Putnam Inc.
375 Hudson Street
New York, NY 10014

Library of Congress Cataloging-in-Publication Data

Monahan, Molly.
Seeds of grace : a nun's reflections on the spirituality
of Alcoholics Anonymous / Molly Monahan.
p.   cm.
ISBN 1-57322-175-9
1. Alcoholics—Religious life.   2. Alcoholics
Anonymous.   3. Twelve step programs—Religious
aspects—Catholic Church.   4. Spiritual life—Catholic
Church.   5. Monahan, Molly.
I. Title.
BV4596.A48 M64   2001   00-046892
261.8'3229286—dc21

Printed in the United States of America
1   3   5   7   9   10   8   6   4   2

This book printed on acid-free paper. ∞

Book design by Amanda Dewey

To the fellowship of Alcoholics Anonymous
in gratitude for "a second spring."

Contents

The Twelve Steps of Alcoholics Anonymous   ix

The Twelve Traditions of Alcoholics Anonymous   xi

Introduction   1

Meetings: "My Name Is Molly and I'm an Alcoholic"   9

The Program in a Nutshell:
A Meditation on the First Three Steps   33

The Purgative Way: Steps Four Through Ten   45

Sponsorship   63

A Meditation on Grace and the Promises   79

Entering on the Illuminative Way   87

The Illuminative Way, "Sought Through
Prayer and Meditation": The Eleventh Step   97

Entering on the Unitive Way:
A Meditation on Anonymity   111

The Unitive Way, "Having Had
a Spiritual Awakening": The Twelfth Step   119

The Twelve Traditions: A Mustard Seed   131

Second Spring: Sin and Salvation   141

The Lamb of God   155

Religion and Spirituality:
"My Name Is Molly and I'm a Catholic"   163

ƚ

The Twelve Steps of Alcoholics Anonymous

1. We admitted we were powerless over alcohol—that our lives had become unmanageable.

2. Came to believe that a Power greater than ourselves could restore us to sanity.

3. Made a decision to turn our will and our lives over to the care of God *as we understood Him.*

4. Made a searching and fearless moral inventory of ourselves.

5. Admitted to God, to ourselves and to another human being the exact nature of our wrongs.

6. Were entirely ready to have God remove all these defects of character.

7. Humbly asked Him to remove our shortcomings.

8. Made a list of all persons we had harmed, and became willing to make amends to them all.

9. Made direct amends to such people wherever possible, except when to do so would injure them or others.

10. Continued to take personal inventory and when we were wrong promptly admitted it.

11. Sought through prayer and meditation to improve our conscious contact with God, *as we understood Him,* praying only for knowledge of His will for us and the power to carry that out.

12. Having had a spiritual awakening as the result of these steps, we tried to carry this message to alcoholics, and to practice these principles in all our affairs.

The Twelve Traditions of Alcoholics Anonymous

1. Our common welfare should come first; personal recovery depends on A.A. unity.

2. For our group purpose there is but one ultimate authority—a loving God as He may express Himself in our group conscience. Our leaders are but trusted servants; they do not govern.

3. The only requirement for A.A. membership is a desire to stop drinking.

4. Each group should be autonomous except in matters affecting other groups or A.A. as a whole.

5. Each group has but one primary purpose—to carry its message to the alcoholic who still suffers.

6. An A.A. group ought never endorse, finance or lend the A.A. name to any related facility or outside enterprise, lest problems of money, property and prestige divert us from our primary purpose.

7. Every A.A. group ought to be fully self-supporting, declining outside contributions.

8. Alcoholics Anonymous should remain forever nonprofessional, but our service centers may employ special workers.

9. A.A., as such, ought never be organized; but we may create service boards or committees directly responsible to those they serve.

10. Alcoholics Anonymous has no opinion on outside issues; hence the A.A. name ought never be drawn into public controversy.

11. Our public relations policy is based on attraction rather than promotion; we need always maintain personal anonymity at the level of the press, radio and films.

12. Anonymity is the spiritual foundation of all our traditions, ever reminding us to place principles before personalities.

Seeds
of
Grace

Introduction

I ONCE HEARD A JESUIT
assert that when the history of twentieth-century
American spirituality is written, Alcoholics Anonymous
will be judged the most significant spiritual movement
of the era. I am quite sure that he was not a member of
A.A. I am, and have been for over seventeen years. I am
also a Roman Catholic nun, and have been for over forty
years. I am inclined to agree with that Jesuit.

Like him, I was called to a way of life devoted in
very specific ways to the spiritual development of its fol-
lowers. I was trained in the Ignatian method of prayer,

1

and have made week-long retreats every year of my religious life. I have read countless books on spirituality, listened to numerous lectures on every facet of the spiritual life, and have a graduate degree in theology. I have been immersed in the rich Roman Catholic sacramental tradition and am a member of a community of women dedicated to the love of God and of neighbor. I feel privileged to have had these opportunities. They strengthened and refined my faith and my understanding of the spiritual life, of Catholic dogma, and, in graduate studies at a nondenominational divinity school, of other religious traditions.

But none of this prevented me from becoming an alcoholic. And I am certain that without Alcoholics Anonymous, "a spiritual program" as we call it, not only would I not be in recovery, I would be spiritually bereft. If that puzzles you, it has puzzled me too. This book is an exploration of that puzzlement. Besides the precious gift of sobriety, what is it that I find in A.A. that I have not found elsewhere? And how is it that my participation in this fellowship has brought me to realizations about my Christian faith that I never had before?

As I began to look for answers to these questions, I recognized that in my alcoholism I experienced myself as being utterly lost and unable to help (save) myself in a way that I never had before. And in the fellowship of

A.A. I have experienced a uniquely (for me) rescuing and empowering community. On the heels of these experiences, I became aware that, as God has made us, there are some things that we just cannot do alone, that a kind of reciprocity, the kind espoused by A.A., is crucial to my salvation, and in surprising ways. To put it another way, the disease of alcoholism, for me, reveals some basic truths about human nature itself in its sad, lost, and sinful state, and Alcoholics Anonymous reveals some things about what God desires for all of us, alcoholics or not.

Given these premises, I hope that what I have written may be helpful for spiritual seekers of any stripe. I offer here my own reflections on my own experience as an alcoholic and as a believing, practicing Christian. But you don't have to be either to accept my invitation to reflect on your own experience, using this book as a guide to that reflection.

In the first part of the book, I try to present A.A. spirituality, nondenominational and nondogmatic as it is, the way you might experience it if you became a member. What is it about A.A. meetings that makes them essential for attaining sobriety, and what spiritual benefits do they offer? What is it like to go through the Twelve Steps? How do the (corny?) slogans that you see on bumper stickers—"Easy Does It," "A Day at a Time"—function as spiritual tools? Is it true that "feelings don't count," as my novice mistress said, or do they play a large part in sobriety and in our spiritual lives? How does sponsorship work? Is a sponsor a kind of spiritual director? What does A.A. have to say about prayer and meditation? What is the "spiritual awakening" that A.A. promises its members in the Twelve Steps? What are the Twelve Traditions and how do they safeguard the mission and the unity of the fellowship? How is anonymity understood to be "the spiritual foundation of all our traditions"?

Inevitably, given my background, elements of Catholic belief and practice have implicitly informed my answers to these questions. In the sections called "Meditations," however, I explicitly look at A.A. through the lens of the language and concepts of the Christian tradition. For instance, I have explored the Twelve Steps using the ancient threefold division of the spiritual life into the purgative, illuminative, and unitive ways. I hope that these sections clarify A.A. spirituality for the reader as they have for me. They also, in my opinion, give warrant for it as being grounded in long-standing spiritual thought and practice. Far from offering "spirituality lite" to its members, or encouraging self-indulgent navel gazing—as I sometimes see Twelve-Step programs caricatured in the media—I have found that A.A. fosters a solid and selfless spirituality.

And because I think that the disease of alcoholism stands in many ways as an emblem of the human condition writ large, I have emphasized that alcoholism is more than just a physical addiction to alcohol. We in A.A. know it to be a physical, mental, and spiritual disease, the last very much to our point here. And we know that recovery is more than merely not drinking, or being "dry." And that sobriety means peace of mind, freedom, and joy in the service of others.

In the last three chapters, I tackle head-on some of the questions that my experience in A.A. has raised for me as a Christian. These are not questions about the truth of my fundamental Catholic beliefs; I have always believed them to be true They are, rather, questions about how truly I believe what I claim to believe in my profession of faith as a Roman Catholic, the distinction that Cardinal Newman made between real and notional assent to dogma. Given my experience of having been saved in A.A., I was led to ask myself about sin and how truly I know myself saved from it. And to wonder how Jesus Christ, who necessarily figures not at all in A.A. spirituality, fits into this picture as my savior. I examine then the differences between religion and the spirituality that A.A. offers, and describe how, far from being in opposition to one another, the two fit together in my life.

Let me say a few words about the subtitle of this book, "Reflections on the Spirituality of Alcoholics Anonymous." I trust that I have made it clear that the book is not intended primarily for members of A.A. Quite the contrary. They don't need to read my book on A.A. spirituality; they have the real thing at their disposal in the fellowship, the Twelve-Step program, and the literature that A.A. provides. They would know, too, as I hope that non-A.A. readers will come to understand, that I am not claiming in any way to speak for A.A. as a whole, or to give a definitive rendering of A.A. spirituality. No one can make those claims. Each A.A. member is free to find the spirituality—a relationship with a Higher Power or the God of his or her understanding—that works for him or her.

When I began to think about this book, I was cautioned against writing "institutional hagiography," that is, a starry-eyed, uncritical account of Alcoholics Anonymous. The person who gave me that advice, like most readers of this book, does not know me personally. Those who do would think the advice unnecessary. I am a Virgo in the signs of the zodiac, a Number One on the Enneagram, and have worked as an editor; I am by temperament, training, and profession, therefore, critical, demanding, a perfectionist. I can drive myself and others crazy with these tendencies. I am as aware of the imperfections of A.A., especially in my own home group, as I am of my own.

Still, I have taken the admonition seriously and have done my best to follow it. If I have erred (I would like to think, on the side of the angels), it is because I am so grateful for the overwhelming benefits and blessings that A.A. has brought me, not least among them learning how to deal with the very character defects mentioned above.

Meetings

"My Name Is Molly and I'm an Alcoholic"

Imagine yourself coming to your first A.A. meeting and saying that sentence with your own name in it. Really, try to imagine it. For all the information disseminated in recent decades about alcoholism as a disease, coming to a meeting is not like a visit to the doctor or going to a health spa. There is still a stigma attached to the condition, and no one is more aware of it than the alcoholic herself. So, stinging shame for some, as it was for me. For others, as for some of the young Turks in the program, the humiliating admission that they can't drink the way their buddies can. Nor does one come for social reasons, to meet friends or make new ones, like joining a club or attending a singles event. Many people come expecting to see the legendary Bowery bums there. Or worse, like me, they fear they will meet someone they know. It was an irrational fear, I know. The people at meetings would be there for the same reason I was. But just such a fear prompts some newcomers to find meetings out of town, in places where they won't be recognized. Might you do that?

No one comes to A.A. for spiritual enlightenment either. I didn't. After all, I was a nun, and had been for years. I knew I was in trouble spiritually—I could pray hardly at all—but I had not connected this condition with my drinking. I thought that I was experiencing the "dark night of the soul" described by the mystics, and reserved for chosen souls called to the higher states of the contemplative life. What could A.A. teach me about spirituality? Going to meetings did not feel like going to church, or going on a retreat, or sitting at the feet of some guru in pursuit of lofty spiritual goals. It felt like defeat to me, as it does for most.

As a matter of fact, I have found all of these benefits in A.A.—the ability not to drink and physical recovery from overindulgence in alcohol; friendship; and a solid and realistic spirituality. But I came to A.A. only from "a desire to stop drinking," the blessedly single requirement that the

Third Tradition of Alcoholics Anonymous lays down for membership in this fellowship of oddly chosen souls.

I am not going to tell my drinking story in any detail here. That is not the point. It is, anyway, a rather tame story compared to some, given any dramatic edge at all by the simple fact of my being a nun. I drank occasionally, socially, as a teenager and a college student. And for the first ten years of my religious life, the time before Vatican II, I drank hardly at all; wine was served in the convent only on Holy Thursday in a ritualized evening meal. After Vatican II, when things loosened up in the convent, happy hours ("preprandials," as the Jesuits call them) became customary in some of the communities I lived in, and I was a moderate partaker, but very early on a faithful one. I did not drink much but I drank regularly.

My drinking picked up in the seventies. I had been teaching in the religious studies department at the college sponsored by my religious community. Then in 1973, for reasons that I did not fully understand, my teaching contract at the college was not renewed. I was offered a position on the college campus ministry team, but I chose not to accept it. Instead, taking advantage of the freedom that nuns had after Vatican II to engage in ministries outside of their communities, I looked for and found exciting work on the staff of an interreligious organization devoted to the place of religion in higher education. It was a high-pressure job. I did a lot of traveling; ate out a lot, joining my colleagues (all male, as it happened) in a Scotch before dinner and wine during it; attended conferences and enjoyed the bibulous socializing that accompanies such events. Then, whether out of town or not and even after I left this work, I was a daily drinker; I could not go for one day, try though I might, without drinking. And then not just one or two, but drinks before dinner, with it, at night when I couldn't sleep, and at times during the day. But "it isn't how much you drink that counts, it's what it does to you," as we say in A.A. Alcohol was doing dreadful things to me, and I began to realize it.

The drug is, after all, a depressant. And I lived during the last years of my drinking with a pervasive, ever-growing, dull ache of sadness, like a deep wound inside that nothing could touch, not therapy, not spiritual direction, nothing. Critical by nature and by academic training, I became negative, querulous, judging others harshly while entertaining grandiose notions of myself. With close friends I grew to be unhealthily dependent on the one hand and demanding and controlling on the other. My emotions were like an infected sore, sensitive to the slightest touch of perceived offense.

I was bewildered and felt myself an utter failure. What had happened to the ideals of discipline and self-sacrifice that I had embraced so ardently on entering the convent? I betrayed them daily. Where was the faith that had inspired me to become a nun and that had sustained me for two decades, even amidst the turmoil of changes in the church and in vowed religious life after Vatican II? Why could I not pray, I, who had longed above all for a life of prayer and union with God?

One reason prayer was impossible for me, I learned in A.A., was because I could not concentrate for any length of time, a direct result of the physiological effects of too much alcohol on my brain. But the malady went deeper than that, as I also learned in A.A. "My spirit was dead," I heard a man say at a meeting. I knew that he was describing me. And I knew then that alcoholism is indeed a soul-sickness which eats away at the innermost fiber of our being. As the disease progressed on all fronts and as my efforts not to drink failed again and again, I was filled with remorse, shame, and, finally, self-loathing. I had never experienced such a feeling before, and, mercifully, have not since. I felt dirty, filthy, inside; I was hopeless and helpless. I could not help myself.

In desperation, in January 1983, I secretly arranged to see a nun who was, and is, an alcoholism counselor. I told her how much I was drinking, hoping against hope that she would tell me that I didn't have a problem. Instead, she asked me only one question: Did I want to go for in-patient or out-patient treatment? And thus it was that four days later I found myself in a twenty-eight-day rehab. I have always been grateful to the superior of my community, who arranged this for me as soon as I told her what was going on. Not only did I feel incapable of not drinking on my own, but the education I got there convinced me of what I was up against in my struggle with alcohol, described as "cunning, baffling, powerful" in the book *Alcoholics Anonymous* (commonly referred to as "The Big Book").

If you think that the disease of alcoholism is just a question of drinking too much and perhaps of behaving badly, even often, you are wrong. A.A. itself is careful to distinguish between social drinking, heavy drinking, and alcoholic drinking, and it makes it quite clear that only the person herself can tell the difference. No, alcoholism is, as the founders of A.A. knew decades before the body/soul connection was being made in medicine and psychology, a threefold disease: a physical, mental (including emotional), and *spiritual* disease, the last to our point here.

We were taught about all of these aspects in rehab. But it was only the notion of alcoholism as a physical disease that impressed me and that I took away with me. I was not ready to deal with the other aspects. A.A. wisdom has it that the disease progresses by affecting us first spiritually, then mentally, and finally physically, and that recovery happens in the opposite order. So it took some time before I became aware of the spiritual effects of alcoholism in myself and of the spiritual benefits of the program. And longer still before I began to reflect on both as I shall do in this book.

Back then, a very shaky and confused beginner, the only thing I knew was that I couldn't stop drinking on my own. The people at rehab stressed attendance at A.A. meetings as essential for recovery. Ninety meetings in ninety days, they said, the advice given to every A.A. beginner. At first I thought the suggestion preposterous, out of all proportion, demanding too much of me and my time, and I said so. Well before the end of my treatment, I was convinced of its value, and would have gone to 180 meetings in ninety days, if that's what it took. Some people do just that.

My commitment to meetings was tested while I was still in rehab. I received a call from a former colleague at the interreligious organization, asking me to be part of an evaluation project involving certain colleges and universities in the Episcopal diocese of Virginia. Grateful for his confidence in me, I accepted, with the humiliating proviso that I could attend A.A. meetings while there. He didn't see any problem with that. So, several weeks after I left the rehab, very newly sober and very scared, I flew to Virginia, rented a car, and spent my first day at a prominent Southern university. I was to stay overnight with a young married faculty member, and was warmly welcomed by him and his wife into their lovely home. It was simply furnished with polished hardwood floors, and strains of Bach were floating through the house from the stereo.

I don't know what they were thinking when I got up from dinner to leave for my meeting, which, at the request of my colleague, they had located for me in a nearby town. I was prepared for this humiliation, carried it off with some bravado, and found my way in the little red rented car to the small church. I wasn't prepared for what happened next. The first person I saw when I entered the meeting room was a man I had met that day at the university, a highly respected professor in the law school, a dedicated teacher and committed Christian. I lost my breath, felt as if I had been stabbed—with hot and piercing and shocking shame. I sat through the meeting with my face burning, worrying about what I would say to this man afterwards, and didn't hear a thing that was said.

But Marcus came up to me as soon as the meeting ended and said, "I knew there was something about you that I liked," such a graceful and understanding greeting that it soothed my shame and established an immediate bond between us. As I found out from him then, in that locale they allow relatives of alcoholics to attend meetings—A.A. and AlAnon together, as it were—and he was there with and because of his wife, and had found his own spirituality there. In the years since 1983, our mutual interests have brought us together at several conferences, and we have talked on the telephone a half dozen times. The bond is always there, a subtext of trust and affection to whatever business matter we are discussing.

Why, you may ask, all of this emphasis on meetings? What is it about meetings that made it possible for me to stop drinking, made, and makes, the impossible possible for millions of alcoholics? There is no full answer to that question. It remains something of a mystery. But for a first inkling of what it might be, we have to go back to the very beginning of Alcoholics Anonymous. There, I believe, is a story that reveals a deep truth not only about alcoholics and alcoholism but about all of us in our various woes.

In the first chapter of "The Big Book" entitled "Bill's Story," Bill Wilson, who, with Dr. Bob Smith, was cofounder of Alcoholics Anonymous, tells us about himself. He was a bright man, successful on Wall Street—and a disastrous drunk, who lost everything more than once because of his drinking. He had been hospitalized, more than once, for the disease of alcoholism; had been intermittently dry for longer or shorter periods but, inevitably, it seemed to him, he always began drinking again.

During a long visit with an old friend, an alcoholic who credited his newly found sobriety to the power of God, Bill came to his own understanding of a God personal to him. He began to believe that this God could help him stop drinking. Then, in the hospital where he had gone for treatment of delirium tremens, Bill was separated from alcohol forever. There too, with the help of God and his friend, he entered into a process of spiritual and moral conversion, culminating in a "sudden and profound" experience of God. "There was a sense of victory, followed by such a peace and serenity as I had ever known." Filled with gratitude for what had freely been given to him through the intervention of his friend, he realized that to stay sober "it was imperative to work with others as [his friend] had worked" with him. This realization crystallized for him in the event that is taken to be the founding of Alcoholics Anonymous.*

---

*Bill does not tell us so in this chapter, but it is well known that his friend was a recent convert to the Oxford Group, the name that the movement in the United States adopted for itself in 1928. A twentieth-century non-denominational evangelical fellowship, it stressed the principles of self-examination, admission of sins, restitution for them, and the service of others, just the principles that Bill embraced in the hospital. They are contained in modified form in the Twelve Steps of A.A., as we shall see. A.A. began its life within the Oxford Group, and after several years diverged from it in disagreement over the group's insistence on absolute ideals of behavior and practice. It was found that absolutes just didn't work for alcoholics.

A few months out of the hospital and still shakily sober, Bill was in the Mayflower Hotel in Akron, Ohio, on a Saturday night in June 1935. The hotel bar was crowded, warm and tempting laughter from it drifting into the lobby, where Bill paced back and forth, resisting the urge to go in and have a drink. Instead, he turned the other way and went to a nearby phone booth, picked out the name of a minister from the ministers' directory there, and began making phone calls to find a fellow drunk. Remembering his own experience, he knew that he needed to talk to another drunk in order to keep from drinking himself. His tenth call was to the woman who arranged for him to meet Dr. Bob, an Akron surgeon, deep in the throes of the disease. The two met, and A.A. was born. A fateful, providential choice: If Bill had gone to the bar instead of the phone booth, where might the millions of alcoholics who have been helped by the program be? Where might I be?

He needed to talk to another drunk in order to keep from drinking himself. Don't you think that this is extraordinary? That this should be a remedy for a disease that had stumped physicians for centuries, defeating every kind of imaginable treatment, some well founded, some wacky, until most doctors and everybody else had given up on the disease and its sufferers? But there it is. The beginning of A.A. meetings and of the mysterious way that A.A. works: talking to another drunk.

And there it is, the deeper truth—that we need to help others in order to be helped ourselves, and not just with the disease of alcoholism. I can only think that this reciprocity must be a God-given part of our nature, our true nature, but obscured for us by the illusion of isolation and of independence and by a misguided selfishness.

You could think of ninety meetings in ninety days as a kind of catechumenate, a place where, especially if you have not been to a rehab, you begin to learn the basics about the disease of alcoholism and about the fellowship of Alcoholics Anonymous. The chair of the meeting begins by asking if there are any newcomers or visitors or "people who are coming back" present, and if there are, they are welcomed. Newcomers are advised to stay after the meeting, get some phone numbers, join a group, and get a temporary sponsor. Usually the two brief paragraphs that describe A.A.'s purpose and principles—called the Preamble—are read:

Alcoholics Anonymous is a fellowship of men and women who share their experience, strength, and hope with each other that they may solve their common problem and help others to recover from alcoholism.

The only requirement for membership is a
desire to stop drinking. There are no dues or
fees in A.A. We are self-supporting through our
own contributions. A.A. is not allied with any
sect, denomination, politics, organization, or
institution; does not wish to engage in any controversy; neither endorses nor opposes any
causes. Our primary purpose is to stay sober
and help other alcoholics to achieve sobriety.

It is difficult to convey a sense of what goes on at A.A.
meetings. I have never seen anything in the movies or on
TV that comes close to capturing it. Since every A.A.
group is autonomous, an array of different kinds of meetings is offered in each group, most of them closed, that is,
for A.A. members or prospective members only: beginners' meetings, men's meetings, women's meetings, and
step meetings. There are topic meetings, where the leader
chooses a theme for the meeting like fear, or gratitude, or
one of the slogans; meetings where A.A. literature—most
often, the books *Alcoholics Anonymous* and *Twelve Steps
and Twelve Traditions* (the latter generally referred to as
"The Twelve and Twelve")—are read and/or talked about;
Eleventh-Step meditation meetings, with a period for
silent group prayer followed by sharing; and open meetings, which anyone is free to attend, with guest speakers

from another group taking up the hour. In my group, anniversary meetings are held on the last Thursday of each month with a candlelit cake, the singing of "Happy Anniversary . . . dear celebrants," brief testimonies from those whose anniversary it is, and cake and coffee afterwards. In celebration of people who got sober in that month, they are also open, often with family members and friends in attendance.

Each group has its own practices, too, and its own personality, as it were, the tough love of one distinguishing it from the easy ways of another. Some groups, for instance, don't allow newcomers to speak; others encourage them to. One of the advantages of attending daily meetings for ninety days is that newcomers are compelled to visit different groups and so are helped to find the group that has what they need. In my part of the country, there are dozens of meetings every day, morning, noon, and night, within easy driving distance.

For all the differences, however, there is a basic pattern underlying meetings. Most are just one hour long, start and end promptly on the minute, and, after the preliminaries, begin with someone telling a bit of her story. She discloses "in a general way," as "The Big Book" advises, what she used to be like, what happened, and what she is like now. Then, speaking briefly on a topic of her choice, or about a certain step, or about a reading that has been done together, she goes around the room, inviting others to speak. The one leading the meeting may be the youngest person in the room, or the least prepossessing. It doesn't matter. "We are all only one drink away from a drunk," we say. Or put another way, "The person in the room with the most sobriety is the one who got up earliest today."

In my group, as in most, there is little cross-talk. That is, only the speaker may comment now and then on what is said by other members. (In this way, A.A. is different from other kinds of support groups where free exchange and feedback are essential.) One may speak briefly, or, in a large meeting, not at all. Since every A.A. group is self-supporting, and there are no dues or fees, the basket is passed to cover expenses—for rent, the purchase of A.A. literature, celebrations, coffee, etc. The customary offering is one dollar, making A.A. without doubt the cheapest therapy going. The meeting ends with a prayer or a moment of silence offered for those still suffering from the disease of alcoholism.

If not in my first ninety days, then very early on, I recognized several valuable things about A.A. meetings. The first was that more often than not I was hearing a startling kind of truth. Not dogmatic, or mathematical, or scientific truth, certainly. No, what I heard at meetings was personal truth, arising out of the experience of the speakers. It was a kind of "witnessing," a practice common in some of the more evangelical churches, but done here in what I would call an austere manner, briefly, and as indicated above, in a general way. The truth I heard was not so much in the details of how much people drank, or what they suffered or lost as a result of their drinking, though it is always salutary to hear that, a way of keeping the memory of my own drinking green. Rather, I heard the truth of my own feelings, faults, and sneaky motivations played back for me with uncommon honesty. And I began to know that I was not alone, and that I was not unique. That is what the suggestion "Identify, don't compare," often given at the beginning of meetings, means.

Like most beginners, I was anxious about what I would say when it came my turn to speak, nervous about what people would think of me. Gradually, I learned that the absence of cross-talk both protected me from overt criticism and gave me no cause for wasting time in an imagined rebuttal to what others said. So the challenge put to me by their honest disclosure, not only about their drinking and how the program worked for them, but about themselves, warts and all, was an interior one. My only task was to figure out what I really felt and thought and then to say it as clearly as I could. No small task that, and more helpful to me than any amount of criticism.

And I learned that meetings calmed me, brought me peace. In those early days, I was an emotional mess. No longer beset with the obsession to drink, I was plagued by—trapped in—the obsessions of negative thinking, hurt feelings, anger, remorse, shame, a sense of failure. But I discovered that if I really listened at meetings, I was free of those sick preoccupations for at least as long as the meeting lasted. And if I did not stir them up afterwards, I was okay for the rest of the day or night. Even today, after seventeen years in the program, if I miss meetings for any period of time, those bad old habits begin to reassert themselves; I am likely to be caught again in "stinking thinking," as we call it. And once I get back to meetings, I am restored to sanity and to peace. Why is this so?

As best I can figure out now, these beneficent results come from listening. By my reckoning, even if one shares at a meeting, which is not always the case, more than 95 percent of every meeting with twenty or more people in attendance is spent listening. That is, roughly, in inverse proportion to the time a client spends talking and listening in most psychotherapies, where talking and being listened to is thought to be the cure; we have become accustomed to thinking that this is how healing takes place. And that happens, too, at A.A. meetings, the difference being that one speaks so little and that one is listened to by a motley group, not a trained professional. Still, it seems to do us good. And at times, when something especially difficult or painful has been shared, the atmosphere in the room changes. The silence and attentiveness and caring become palpable; I can feel them in the room as a presence. It is as if the one suffering is being held in a quiet, communal embrace. And it is powerfully healing.

But listening itself? And to a bunch of drunks? It strikes me as very strange. The most obvious explanation is the one I gave above: For a period of time, one is released from the squirrel cage of one's own thoughts about one's own all-important self, which is a blessed relief. More deeply, however, it may be the case that Bill's insight is at work here too. The so-called St. Francis prayer, which figures prominently in A.A. spirituality, asks: "Lord, grant that I may seek rather to comfort than to be comforted—to understand, than to be understood—to love, than to be loved. For it is by self-forgetting that one finds. It is by forgiving that one is forgiven. It is by dying that one awakens to Eternal Life."

It is by listening to others in an attentive, healing way that one is healed.

So yes, A.A. is a kind of psychotherapy, though that is not all it is. It also offers a good amount of drama, both tragedy and comedy. There is a lot of laughter at meetings, sometimes because the person speaking has the comic gift, more often because what is shared makes us laugh—at ourselves. At a meeting I attended earlier this year, a young Jewish therapist, from an Orthodox family but no longer practicing, was terribly upset. She had been to an event honoring her very successful brother. Every sore spot in her relationship with him and with her family had been touched; she felt slighted, an outsider, the loser in the family. And—she had "only bought a quarter-page ad in the journal. Everyone else in the family had taken a full page." Laughter. A bit stifled out of kindness to our friend. But empathetic laughter at the recognition of those small, really insignificant things that can bother us so much. Been there. Done that. All of us.

I have listened to criminals, erstwhile street people, those who have attempted suicide, and "the ladies who lunch." One of these last, a handsome woman, a grandmother now and active in the local community, told of having once driven to a nearby convenience store at night with her then eight-year-old daughter. She sent the child into the store to buy cigarettes. In a drunken stupor, she forgot why she was there and drove off, leaving the youngster to walk home alone in the dark in her nightgown. This story reveals the ravages that alcoholism can wreak on us and our families better than many a "drunkalogue" I have heard. And I think it took more courage to tell it than if the woman had confessed to having robbed the store.

There are success stories, too, stories with happy endings: skinheads talking about their "spiritual condition"; people who were unemployable when they came in earning college degrees and job promotions; family reconciliations after long estrangements; courageous divorces releasing people from sick and destructive marriages. It is all there, the human condition in all its weal and woe, commonly suffered, commonly enjoyed, commonly shared, by people from every walk of life—upper class, middle class, lower class, young and old, men and women, of different colors, with different accents, from different religious backgrounds. Where else would I, an academically trained nun, have found the opportunity to meet and know such a variety of people as intimately as I do? It may sound crass to say it, but I find it enormously interesting, and heartening.

This is one answer to the questions that people not in the program sometimes ask about meetings. "Aren't they boring? Doesn't it get boring after years of attendance?" Yes, meetings can on occasion be boring. Some people tend to talk too much. Some say the same thing every time they speak. Some few promote their own thinly disguised egos, so thinly disguised it makes me wonder that they do not see their egotism themselves. (Then that makes me wonder, Do I do that?) But I have seldom heard a bad speaker in A.A. Even after initial admissions of nervousness at speaking before a large group—at some open meetings there can be more than one hundred people in attendance—when people get into their own stories they are almost invariably engaging. All of us, after all, are experts when speaking on the topic of ourselves.

Or, thinking that A.A. is just about drinking and knowing that I no longer drink, people ask why I keep going to meetings. As I said earlier, I need to go to keep my thinking straight. And, following Bill Wilson, I need to go to be there for others, an essential part of my own recovery. If every recovering member of A.A. no longer went to meetings, there wouldn't be any meetings.

The meetings that I usually attend are held in church basements, meeting rooms, or classrooms. (The fact that the rooms are not very attractive or that the seats are not very comfortable doesn't seem to bother anyone.) But they can take place anywhere—in hospitals, community centers, people's homes.

For the last several years some women in my group have brought a meeting to Kay in her apartment. Kay had finally gotten the program after many, many slips and more than twenty institutionalizations. Then, not an old woman, she suffered a debilitating stroke, making it very difficult for her to come to meetings. So the meetings come to her.

Or, to give another example, here is a story I heard several months ago from a good-looking, soft-spoken older man in our group. He had been on a plane a few days earlier when the flight attendant asked over the speaker whether there were any "friends of Bill Wilson" aboard, and if so, would they come to the back of the plane. He responded immediately, as did five other passengers. They found a young woman there who was on her way to a rehab; she was afraid she would drink on the plane. It was a perfect setting and she had a perfect "excuse" for drinking, as any alcoholic would immediately recognize. She was alone, unknown; it was a chance for one last fling. They stayed with her for the rest of the flight. She went off to the rehab sober, and with her resolve not to drink and her self-respect intact. I think that is a wonderful story, wonderful for the young woman, wonderful for the people who came to her aid, wonderfully encouraging for the rest of us to hear.

I am aware that I have not explained exactly how it is that going to meetings enables people to stop drinking. I don't know. And I don't know if anybody does. For some, the desire to drink is lifted from them at their first meeting. Others struggle with it for months, or longer. A woman celebrating her twenty-second anniversary this week told of having been obsessed with the desire to drink for four days earlier this year. Some people come in and out of the program over and over again. They are always warmly welcomed back, never berated. Some of them reach lasting sobriety. Some, tragically, never do.

Mindful of the last, sober A.A. members who have been able to stop drinking and to "stay stopped," as we say, often speak of themselves as "chosen," of having received sobriety as a gift. I believe that I have indeed received a gift, but my conviction that God loves everyone and desires good for everyone keeps me from thinking of myself as chosen. I simply do not know why I am among those who are fortunate enough to be in recovery.

And that is how it works, just the way it worked for Bill Wilson. "It *works* if you *work* it, so *work* it, you're *worth* it!"—one of A.A.'s damned (true) sayings. We recite it in chorus at the end of some meetings, holding hands and pumping them up and down on each of the four beats. Well, no, that is *one* of the ways A.A. works.

Meetings are not the whole program. But coming to them is essential for what follows. And what follows is hinted at in another saying, "Came, came to, came to believe," which points to the first three of the now famous Twelve Steps.

The Program in a Nutshell

A Meditation on the
First Three Steps

STEP ONE: "WE ADMITTED
we were powerless over alcohol—that our lives had
become unmanageable." Step Two: "Came to believe
that a Power greater than ourselves could restore us to
sanity." Step Three: "Made a decision to turn our will
and our lives over to the care of God *as we* [each of us]
understood Him." It is only now, as I have been thinking
about the first three steps, pondering how much they ask
of us—so soon and yet so gently—that I have begun to
realize two things about them. One, they anticipate—
encapsulate, as it were—the rest of the Twelve Steps.

And two, what they lay out, and what the entire program plays out, can be seen to correspond to the ancient
Christian description of growth in the spiritual life
known as the purgative, illuminative, and unitive ways.

The First Step makes no mention of God at all,
appealing as it does only to the very concrete experience
of our powerlessness over alcohol (the physical aspect of
the disease, our addiction) and of the unmanageability of
our lives. Unmanageability is a gentle way of referring to
the mess we have made of things, the character defects
that we suffer from, the harm that we have done to ourselves and to others, the very things that are dealt with in
Steps Four through Ten.

The Second Step offers the first gleam of spiritual
light by pointing to an inchoate faith in an as-yet-
unnamed Power. And, by inference, the phrase "could
restore us to sanity" indicates that there is something
seriously wrong with our thinking, not only with our
actions. We are in a state of confusion and darkness (the
mental aspect of the disease) and in need of the light
(illumination) that will come to us as, in Step Eleven, we
seek "through prayer and meditation to improve our
conscious contact with God . . . praying only for knowledge of His will for us and the power to carry that out."

The Third Step, using the word "God" for the first
time, asks us to make a great leap of faith, no less than

that of turning our will and our lives over to the God of our understanding. Until now, even if we were believers, we have lived as functional atheists (the spiritual aspect of the disease), acting as if we were in charge of things, and as if no one would take care of us if we did not take care of ourselves. We certainly had only a minute amount of trust and love. The turning over in Step Three asks us to surrender to God, and it had better be a God of love. It prepares the ground for the spiritual awakening promised in Step Twelve.

If you are familiar with the traditional stages of the spiritual life that I mentioned above, you may already see what I saw only the day before yesterday: an outline of the purgative, illuminative, and unitive ways. If you are not, let me explain them and their relationship to the steps briefly here.

The purgative way is generally understood to describe the stage of beginners in the spiritual life. Derived from the word "purge," with its connotations of cleansing, purifying, clearing of guilt, and, in medical language, of the evacuation of the bowels, the term indicates that the attention and energy of beginners be directed to acknowledging and turning away from sin in all its noxious effects. As articulated in the steps, the purgative way calls for dealing with the unmanageability mentioned in Step One. We do this by making "a fearless and searching moral inventory" in Step Four, and by admitting "to God, to ourselves and to another human being the exact nature of our wrongs" in Step Five. In Steps Six through Ten, we see that the wrongs we have done are rooted in our character defects, and we willingly and humbly ask God to remove our shortcomings; we can no more tackle these on our own than we could stop drinking. We willingly make amends to those we have harmed. We remain vigilant in our spiritual lives by continuing "to take personal inventory" and promptly admitting when we are wrong. These steps, in short, engage us in a process of purgation, of conversion.

"The second, the illuminative stage, was one of deepening knowledge and love of God within a contemplative experience," writes Philip Sheldrake in *The HarperCollins Encyclopedia of Catholicism* article "The Ways of the Spiritual Life." This will be the goal of the Eleventh Step as we seek "through prayer and meditation to improve our *conscious* (italics mine) contact with God . . . praying only for knowledge of His will for us and the power to carry that out." We are very far from any such desires in Step Two. But a little seed of belief in a Power greater than ourselves—our only hope in the face of our own acknowledged powerlessness over alcohol—has been planted by this step.

And it is this Power, says Step Two, that can restore us to sanity. Most of us simply cannot see our insanity at first or don't want to admit to it when we do; I bridled at the mere mention of the word. At some point, however, we can no longer deny that we *have* been insane in our obsession with alcohol and our compulsive drinking, and in the crazy and harmful things they led us to think and say and do. Far from having any claim to wisdom or enlightenment, we have been wanting in common soundness of mind. (I am reminded as I write this of the women who related, with sober horror, that they sometimes drove their children's car pool when intoxicated.)

So we have to clear up mentally before we have the capacity for the prayer and meditation mentioned in the Eleventh Step. Gradually, we gain the ability to concentrate, freedom from obsessive thinking, and some degree of peace, all necessary conditions for a life of prayer By the time we reach Step Eleven, we will have begun to understand that we have been living in the fundamental illusion—the opposite of enlightenment—that *we* are all-knowing and all-powerful; we have indeed been trying to play the part of God ourselves. We want now to come to better know and love the gracious and healing Power which has brought us these blessings, and we at least glimpse the wisdom of praying "only for the knowledge of [God's] will for us and the power to carry that out." We have moved from darkness to light, the illuminative way.

Finally, we come to the unitive way and the Third and Twelfth Steps. Step Twelve reads: "Having had a spiritual awakening as a result of these steps, we tried to carry this message to other alcoholics and to practice these principles in all our affairs." The A.A. literature on Step Twelve makes no mention of the highest states of mystical prayer and union with God traditionally associated with the unitive way. But the summary of this stage of the spiritual life in *The Encyclopedia of Catholicism* strikes a less esoteric, though no less profound, note. It describes the unitive way as one in which "desire is dominated by love of God *and of all things in God*" (italics mine). The love of God, it seems, is not a purely private affair to be enjoyed in moments of private contemplation or for ourselves alone. Of its nature, because "God is love," as the Christian scriptures say (1 Jn. 4:8), and loves all that God has made, it reaches out to embrace all.

Now, in the Twelfth Step, having had a spiritual awakening, we see that the decision, the leap of faith, made in the Third Step, "to turn our will and our lives over to the care of God," means that our lives are at the service of others. At the time we took the Third Step, we only made a decision, a decision that was initially carried out in our willingness to go on with the rest of the steps. Now, we see that the love to which we entrusted our will and our lives is meant to bear fruit in action as we try, in the last step, "to carry this message to alcoholics, and to practice these principles in all our affairs." A life of love and service. The unitive way.

This traditional division of the spiritual life into absolutely distinct phases may seem too rigid to you, as it does to many contemporary spiritual writers and practitioners in the Christian tradition. Each of us, as A.A. so clearly acknowledges, has a unique relationship with God. We find our own way to God in our (and God's) own time, and sometimes by very circuitous routes. Further, we are at *every* point in the journey called in some way to "conversion, enlargement of vision, and growth in selfless love," as Sheldrake says.

Assuming that my interpretation of the first three steps as containing in seedlike fashion all that is to follow has validity, the founders of A.A. somehow had the wisdom to know this. They recognized some basic truths about human beings and human life. They understood that life is a process. We don't know at the beginning of any major venture, the making of any major decision in life—like the decision made in the marriage vows "to have and to hold in sickness and in health, in riches and poverty"— what will be asked of us. Further, *we* are in process; we don't have the same resources at the beginning of the venture that we will have as we change and grow. As long as we are alive we are never finished, never perfect, the project of our lives never completed. "The Big Book" captures this hard-won wisdom in its statement that "we claim spiritual progress rather than spiritual perfection." But the founders were also wise enough to know that if we do not make as wholehearted a commitment as we are capable of at the very outset, we are not likely to succeed.

The poor befuddled beginner has no notion of any of this. The "came to" in "Came, came to, came to believe" refers not so much to any kind of spiritual enlightenment as to clearing up the very real distortions in thinking that characterize the mental aspects of the disease of alcoholism. In fact, beginners are counseled, "Don't think, don't drink, and come to meetings," and "Utilize, don't analyze." As "The Big Book" says, "The spiritual life is not a theory. *We have to live it.*" And the initial steps in living it are made as easy as possible for us.

I have always thought that the adoption of the phrases "Higher Power" and "God, *as we understood Him,*" were strokes of genius—or divine inspiration—on the part of A.A.'s founders. Think of the terrible divisions within Christianity over matters dogmatic, of the destruction and death it has wrought on others in wars, inquisitions, pogroms. Think of the persecution of "unbelievers" in the name of whatever religion, even today. These phrases undergird the A.A. principle that "the only requirement for membership is a desire to stop drinking," making the fellowship available to everyone, regardless of religious (or any other) persuasion. Along with the operating principles found in the Twelve Traditions, these phrases safeguard the internal unity of the fellowship in its matter-of-life-and-death mission to every suffering alcoholic. Thousands of people do die every year from this disease. Just as the heart surgeon does not ask the patient on the table about her religious convictions, so neither does A.A. ask prospective members about theirs.

For those who have not yet come to a belief in God, or those who are atheists by conviction, the group itself, or anything else, may serve as a Higher Power. As long as the self is no longer considered omnipotent, it seems to work. For those alienated from the religion of their upbringing, unsure of their faith, or who have never had any religious training at all, the phrase "as we understood Him" provides the needed leeway to the recovery or the beginnings of faith.

Both phrases show the deep respect for the freedom of the individual that runs as a leitmotif through the entire program of A.A., and both recognize that if faith is to be genuine, it must be grounded in the experience of the person. Faith here does not mean belief in some dogma or abstract principle to which one pays lip service or gives a kind of disembodied intellectual assent. It means a lived truth. Because of a faith that works, that has been experienced as efficacious, most alcoholics do come to believe in a loving, caring God.

In fact, when my faith in my Catholic religion, and sometimes even in the existence of God, is weak, my experience in A.A. comes to my rescue. I can literally see and hear the effects of faith in a roomful of people whose trust in a Higher Power has restored them to health of body, mind, and soul. And that is just how it works for the beginner. No one proselytizes, no one insists on any belief. The beginner, and all of us at different times, is carried along by the faith of others. "I wanted what you people have," beginners often say, meaning, first of all, sobriety. And then they are told, "Don't leave before the miracle happens," meaning, a spiritual awakening. It sounds corny, doesn't it, until you remember who is saying it—people who were morally and spiritually bankrupt, many of whom never dreamed that they would want or could have anything like a spiritual life.

I don't remember even noticing the mention of a spiritual awakening during my first years in A.A. I do recall smarting under a description of the alcoholic personality that I found in "The Twelve and Twelve." A group of eminent psychologists and doctors had concluded from a study when A.A. was quite young "that most of the alcoholics under investigation were still childish, emotionally sensitive, and grandiose." Why did these words sting, except that they offered an accurate description of myself at that point? So I had to grow up, find some emotional stability, and become "right-sized," "teachable," the phrases that many A.A.s use for humility. Far from being tested in some esoteric dark night of the soul, as I had thought, I was a beginner in *every* sense of the word. I was setting out on the purgative way.

The Purgative Way

Steps Four Through Ten

LIKE MOST PEOPLE IN LATE twentieth-century America, I must have had some vague notion of alcoholism as a disease before I began drinking alcoholically. But that's all it was—a vague notion, and it didn't help at all with the shame I felt when I finally acknowledged my condition. At the rehab, where I began to learn about the physiological, mental/emotional, and spiritual aspects of the disease—and I suffered from all of them—I conceded the validity of the concept and the accuracy of the diagnosis in my case. It helped some, but not a lot, in diminishing my shame.

Gradually, I embraced the concept with some relief. I was not a bad person, a weak person. I was a sick person.

In the way that A.A. understands and "treats" alcoholism, however, admitting that you have a disease doesn't let you off the hook. It doesn't absolve you from taking responsibility for the person you were when you were drinking or for the things that you did. You cannot use your disease as an excuse. Once you admit that you are powerless over alcohol, your recovery depends on getting into action. Far from the comforting bromide "I'm OK, you're OK," the program tells you, in effect, "I'm not OK, you're not OK. But we can get better." Change is required. In spiritual language, conversion—the purgative way. Or, as I once heard someone say at a meeting, "God loves you just the way you are, but too much to let you stay that way."

My sponsor (the steps are usually done under the guidance of a sponsor) delayed my taking Step Four—"made a searching and fearless moral inventory of ourselves"—until I had regained some little degree of self-esteem, a kind and wise judgment in my case. Even so, I was still so full of shame and so conscious of my failure as a nun that I spent most of my time and energy agonizing not over my offenses but over having to tell them to her in Step Five: "Admitted to God, to ourselves, and to another human being the exact nature of our wrongs." So, with her approval, and taking advantage of the utter freedom that the program espouses—"The Twelve and Twelve" allows for doing the Fifth Step even with "a complete stranger"—I did this step with a woman I had been seeing for spiritual direction, a person accustomed to dealing with nuns. Hard as it was, doing the Fifth Step with her was easier for me. It was less nakedly personal somehow, rather like talking to a therapist who you know has heard it all before.

People in A.A. do not use the word "sin," but "The Twelve and Twelve" suggests the list of the seven deadly sins—pride, greed, lust, anger, gluttony, envy, sloth—as a help to making our personal inventory in the Fourth Step. At greater length, it examines primary instincts run wild in the drives for sex, money, and power, exactly the substance of what I renounced in my vows of chastity, poverty, and obedience. It does not use the word "confession" either, but the Fifth Step recalls the making of a general confession of one's entire life that I as a young nun was encouraged to make to a priest every year during our annual retreat.

Step Six reads, "Were entirely ready to have God remove all these defects of character," an admittedly elusive step. How do you know when you are entirely ready? Here is how it often works. Earlier this year, I was leading a women's meeting. I forget what the topic was.

At any rate, a young woman in the group spoke up with vehement anger: She hated her parents, she hated her life, she didn't want to change, she was miserably unhappy. Drawing on my experience in A.A., I asked her what step she was on. Sure enough, she was on Step Six. It had brought her to that stage in her spiritual development where she was painfully *aware* of her character defects in a way that she hadn't been before. When the pain got bad enough, and when she realized that she could not free herself from it by her own efforts, she would become ready to turn to God for help, to make a beginning in what A.A. acknowledges is the job of a lifetime, a job that is never completely finished.

In Step Seven, we humbly ask God "to remove our shortcomings." The seven pages devoted to this step in "The Twelve and Twelve" deal almost exclusively with the virtue of humility. Even at the time of writing, in the 1950s, the book acknowledged that "humility, as a word and as an ideal, has a very bad time of it in our world." All the more now, when it—or at least a false version of it—has been disowned by women upon whom it was often foisted as a way of keeping them in their place. The chapter anchors humility first of all in the admission of our powerlessness over alcohol; it is a necessity for us if we are to get and to stay sober. The chapter goes on:

For just so long as we were convinced that we could live exclusively by our own individual strength and intelligence, for just that long was a working faith in a Higher Power impossible. . . . We could actually have earnest religious beliefs which remained barren because we were still trying to play God ourselves.

Playing God is just what I was doing, I realized, in all the "good advice" I was dealing out, unsolicited, to family, friends, sisters. What right did I have, in what my brother-in-law termed "the most depressing conversation" he had ever had, to advise him and my sister on their financial affairs? Did I think that a mere word of mine, spoken to a friend, even with the best of intentions, was powerful enough—like God's at the creation—to change a lifelong pattern of behavior? No, the only thing I could change, as A.A. constantly reminds us, was myself, and that, only with the grace of God. So I became at least humble enough to try to shut up and to offer my counsel only when it was asked for.

In a subtle, perceptive, and refreshingly down-to-earth fashion, the chapter goes on to explore humility as "the avenue to true freedom of the human spirit . . . not humble pie but the nourishing ingredient which can give us serenity . . . a healer of pain." It concludes that in

Step Seven "with humility as our guide, we move out from ourselves toward others and toward God."

We don't talk much about humility in A.A., almost never use the word. Maybe that is because, as the spiritual adage has it, if you think you are humble, you are not. But I see enough of freedom, serenity, healing, and unselfishness around me to think that it must be hiding there somewhere.

Steps Eight and Nine have to do with facing up to all the harm we have done to others, with the willingness to make amends to them, and with making "direct amends to such people wherever possible, except when to do so would injure them or others." No easy apology this last. It might entail, for example, approaching a former spouse after a bitter divorce, or the paying back of bad debts or stolen money. If there is a good reason for not disclosing thefts that have been committed, or no feasible way of returning stolen property, sponsors often advise making donations to an appropriate charity instead. And just as important, this step entails amending—changing—ourselves, our attitudes, and our behavior.

When I first did Step Nine, I was heedless of the oft-repeated admonition that we are to do it for our own sake, regardless of the response of the other person. We are to take responsibility for our part in the situation, to clean up our side of the street, and so rid ourselves of the burden of guilt. But, as I realized later, at least once, my real motive in making amends was to renegotiate the relationship, thus subverting the purpose of the step. It did not work, and I was crushed. More recently, a recurring, troubling memory enabled me to see how I had wronged someone over twenty years ago in a friendship that has since withered. This time, I was quick to make clear in my amends that I was not trying to bring the relationship back to life. And I am at peace about it.

In Step Ten, we continue the practice of examination of conscience and the prompt admission of wrong done. I have found the practice of the latter half of this step especially liberating. It has freed me from those countless, fruitless hours spent in interior self-defense after an unpleasant encounter: If he hadn't . . . I wouldn't have. . . . It is so much easier to take responsibility, quickly, for whatever my part in the situation has been, and to lay the matter to rest, at least in my own head.

This is as rigorous a course of action as anything asked of me as a Catholic or, except in the practice of the vows, in my religious life. Think about it the next time you hear a disparaging comment or joke about Twelve-Step programs and ask yourself whether the speaker, or you yourself, would be willing to go through the process; "A.A. is not for sissies," as we say. The purpose of it all, however, is not self-flagellation, but rather peace and freedom, leading to service—the peace that comes from the humble recognition of our powerlessness and from a clear conscience, and the gradual attainment of freedom from the things that drive us, that drive us crazy, that drive us to drink: a tyrannical ego, anger, guilt, resentment, hurt, failure, and perhaps, above all, fear. In undertaking to go through the steps we have the choice, as an A.A. acronym new to me puts it : *F _ _ _ Everything And Run* or *Face Everything And Recover.*

This is only a bare summary of Steps One through Ten as described in "The Big Book" and more fully in "The Twelve and Twelve." Anyone interested in the spiritual life would do well to read both. For the A.A. member, there is the added, inestimable boon of hearing from other members at step meetings how they did each step, what was hard for them, what benefits they experienced, their feelings before, during, and after each step. Contrary to the assertion of my novice mistress that feelings don't count, feelings are important. They have a lot to do both with the disease of alcoholism and with spirituality.

Here is a story to illustrate what I mean about alcoholism. Sue, a pixie-faced woman in her fifties, had been drinking heavily, alcoholically, especially after the death of her husband. Somehow she managed to stop drinking, and for two miserable years was what we call "a dry drunk." That is, although she was not drinking, she still suffered from all of the "isms" of the disease: negative thinking, self-pity, anger, resentment, depression, controlling behavior, etc. Her therapist recommended that she go to A.A. And she did. And she stayed. And here she was some years later, happy, self-confident, peaceful, leading a meeting. What's noteworthy about that? you might ask.

When it was my turn to speak, I said that I was amazed. First, that someone who was able to stop drinking on her own came to A.A. I am quite sure that if I had been able to get *that* monkey off my back, I never would have become a member of Alcoholics Anonymous. Second, that a therapist recognized the problem and directed her to A.A.; so many therapists (fewer in recent years, it seems to me) fail in this respect, and not only because often enough the client is not honest about her drinking. Third, that the woman took the advice and not only came but stayed.

I tell the story because it, and others like it that I have heard, dramatically illustrates an important fact about alcoholism, one not readily recognized by the public at large even now. The fact is this: Alcoholism is not only about drinking. Some A.A. members say, a bit inaccurately, I think, that drinking is "just a symptom." However, that is not completely true either. Alcoholic drinking is an addiction, a disease, and one that aggravates all of our problems—physical (you can die from it), mental (you can literally lose your mind or memory because of it), and spiritual. Abstinence from alcohol is a *sine qua non* of recovery.

Not drinking in itself, however, does not bring one to sobriety or serenity. To begin to recover requires getting at the reasons behind or underneath our drinking. And by that I do not mean the *excuses* that many of us give: If you had my husband, boss, job, illness, etc., you would drink too. I mean our feelings and the negative attitudes that they engender. "It's a disease of the attitudes," we say. And one of the chief culprits in the kingdom of peace of mind is that sneaky thief, fear. Early on in my A.A. life I noticed how often people spoke of fear—the "self-centered fear of not getting what we want or of losing what we have." I was struck especially by how openly the men in our group spoke of their fears, and wondered if there was any other place in this still-macho world of ours where it was acceptable for men to talk like this.

On the other hand, I was not aware of fear in myself. I am not afraid of things like speaking in public or of being alone in a house at night. I don't have much fear of undertaking possibly dangerous physical feats, and am, in fact, sometimes foolhardy in this regard with three broken arms to show for it—one from falling out of a tree when I was seven, one from diving into shallow water when I was twelve, and the last suffered seven or eight years ago when I turned my back on a big wave at the ocean and got walloped stiff-armed and then broken-armed to the sea floor. So I worried—and this may seem strange to you—that if everybody else was afraid and I was not, maybe I didn't belong in this fellowship which I knew I so desperately needed.

Then one day I "saw" it, saw my fear. The experience of recognition was like my first sight of a real seal in the waters of Penobscot Bay in Maine. At first, I didn't know what I was looking at; I flipped rapidly—it took only a second—through my mental file of pictured creatures until I found the one that matched. "It's a seal!" I said.

Just so, except that the process took longer, the word "fear" became real for me when I recognized that it was the engine that drove most of my close relationships with family, friends, sisters. Fear of not getting what I needed led me, on the one hand, to an unhealthy dependence on others, asking from them more than any human being can give—perfect love and understanding. I was afraid I would lose them if I didn't please them, and so was a people pleaser. On the other hand, I was dominating, controlling, fearing what would happen to them if they did not follow my always omniscient advice about what was best for them. The same fear drives others in matters of health, financial security, power, prestige. Whatever its arena, and in many disguises, it is often at the root of all kinds of things we name as sin—of anger, greed, envy, etc. Come to think of it, it may be the true face of many things that masquerade as virtue, too, like humility, obedience, and meekness.

When my novice mistress told us that feelings don't count, she was encouraging us to overcome our selfishness in the pursuit of a life of virtue, self-denial, and duty. "I don't feel like it" was not to be given any weight at all, nor was "I don't like her." And it is a valid saying, and for everyone, as far as it goes. The world would come to a halt if we did only what we felt like doing, dealt politely only with people we liked. But understood as a general principle of the spiritual, and even of the moral life, it is simply wrong-headed. Our feelings do matter, massively, in our search for meaning and value in our lives. Without them, in both their negative and positive valence—in what we love and hate, desire and shun, rejoice in and sorrow over, admire and despise, hope for and fear—"our knowing and deciding would be paper thin," says Jesuit theologian Bernard Lonergan.

But first you have to recognize them and own them, as I did my fear. Then you have to deal with them. It is how we handle our feelings that counts. Willpower, "muscular Christianity," is of little avail here, as all of us who have tried to conquer our feelings by it alone know.

And so a large part of the spiritual life consists in coming to know ourselves and our feelings, cultivating those that are healthy and appropriate, weeding out or redirecting those that are destructive to ourselves and others.

People in A.A. talk of having drunk *at* their anger, having stuffed their feelings, of having drunk for oblivion from them. And I have heard A.A.s on the road to recovery tell of getting their feelings back, and of being glad to have feelings again, even terribly painful ones. So, yes, we do talk about our feelings, but not, as you might imagine, in a "touchy-feely" way, but in a practical, nuts-and-bolts way. In fact, many of what we call "the tools of the program"—among them the slogans, sayings, and acronyms that some of us confess to having at first found dumb, their repetition boring—have in one way or another to do with feelings. The slogans give us a common language to identify and express our feelings, and ways to act to change them. This is what I think people may mean when they say "I didn't have a clue before I came to A.A. about how to live."

Some of the slogans have to do exclusively with drinking, like the most-often repeated "Don't drink and come to meetings," and, "Keep the cork in the bottle." "It's the first drink that gets you drunk" is a little bit of wisdom tested by those who have tried "having only one or two," maybe successfully for a time, until they find themselves drinking as much or more than they were before they tried their little experiment in controlled drinking.

Other sayings have their origin in advice about not drinking and then get extrapolated to life in general; they give guidance that almost anyone would do well to heed. "A day at a time" guards against the negative projection to which so many of us are prone, and echoes the practice in many of the spiritual traditions about living in the present moment. "HALT," standing for hungry, angry, lonely, tired, signals those states of mind and body when we are in more danger of drinking, or of otherwise acting foolishly. The nouns in "avoid people, places, and things" (what Catholics used to call "occasions of sin") that might lead us to drink—like bars, drinking buddies, certain songs or kinds of music reminiscent of our drinking days—get transposed to stand for the many things besides alcohol over which we are powerless.

"Live and let live," "living life on life's terms," "give time time," "let go and let God," "giving someone free rent in my head" all get at our tendency to try to control, our feelings of anxiety, impatience, fear, frustration, our obsessive thinking. Still others give simple and practical advice toward action to relieve unhealthy thoughts and feelings: "move a muscle, change a thought"; "a problem

shared is a problem halved"; "act as if"; "doing the footwork" and then "turning it over" [to the Higher Power];
"showing up for life"; "doing the next right thing."

I must have heard every one of these sayings thousands of times on the lips of hundreds of people over the
years. In other areas of my life, I experience a strong
reaction against clichéd language and do my utmost to
avoid it myself. For some reason, it doesn't bother me
when I hear it in A.A., maybe because it always comes
directly out of the experience of the person using it—
and because the sayings have worked for me.

Finally, there are practices not yet clothed in a slogan
or saying but which one hears often enough to remember. People tell of having rid themselves of hatred,
resentment, anger, or wounded feelings by praying for
the person who "caused" them to feel that way. How
about that? It is strange that I, who know that Jesus said,
"Pray for those who persecute you" (Mt. 5:44), should
be struck by the newness of this advice. The truth is that
Jesus' words never came home to me until I heard them
on the lips of someone who put the advice into practice.

Jesus also taught us to pray, "Forgive us our tres-
passes as we forgive those who trespass against us." This
past winter at a women's meeting, a mother with teenage
sons told of a difficulty her older son was having with a

friend. She talked to him about forgiveness. "You've got to do it for your own sake," she said. "You'll never be happy unless you learn to forgive others." How many parents are teaching their children about forgiveness the way she was? Not many is my guess.

But like many matters spiritual, forgiveness is easier to talk about than to do. We may believe that forgiving others will bring us peace, but it is easier to say "I forgive you" than it is to *feel* genuine forgiveness. So, how do you do it? That is the question. The little meditation book *Twenty-Four Hours a Day,* which I read every morning before my reflection on the scripture of the day, gave me some good advice. It counseled working at overcoming my selfishness before I even thought of forgiving others. The self-centered "me," quick to take offense and to harbor resentment, should not even think about injuries done to it. When I have overcome, to some degree, my selfishness in daily life, it said, then I will find that "there is nothing in me that remembers injury, because the only thing injured, my selfishness, is gone."

I found this advice startling when I first read it and sensed its truth. It implies for one thing that forgiveness is a process. It takes time. Praying for the person who hurt you is a first step, supposing, as it does, that you *want* to be able to forgive, that you acknowledge the offender as also under God's care, that you wish him or her no evil. Or that you hope your act of prayer will bring you to these dispositions. And I have understood only recently that forgiveness is a process that may or may not entail reconciliation. You may forgive a former spouse, or friend, or family member without necessarily, and for good reason, being restored to any relationship with him or her, let alone the relationship enjoyed before the injury.

This summer during my annual retreat, the directors of the retreat conducted a communal penance service for the retreatants. The service was very carefully and thoughtfully done, not rushed, helping us to go over in our minds different periods in our lives, different relationships and situations. It concluded with our approaching one of the directors and indicating with a few words and a gesture what we wanted to be healed of, forgiven for.

After the service was over, I became aware of an unanticipated effect it had on me. I realized in reviewing my life that I no longer had anything to forgive anyone—no grudges, resentments, memories of pain suffered at the hands of others. I told my director this in my next session alone with her. "Molly," she said, "do you realize what a great grace you've been given?" Well, no, I hadn't, not until she said that, and only as I have reflected on it since. It is a great grace. And it's one that I'm not going to poke around in to try to scare up some lost memory of a past injury in order to test its reality.

In January 2000 I celebrated my seventeenth anniversary in A.A. It took that long—or that little time—to "find that there is nothing in me that remembers injury," as my meditation book promised.

Sponsorship

When I had been in the program for several years, and before I began to sponsor anyone myself, I was witness to this little episode.

Vito looked like a young thug. He talked like a young thug. He probably had been a thug. "Geez!" he said to another young thug, "I'm nervous. I gotta hear Andy's Fifth Step tonight." Geez, I thought to myself, isn't that incredible! He was, no doubt, Andy's sponsor, and was going to hear his "confession," already a pretty startling occurrence, evidence of a dramatic change from what I imagine to have been his way of life. And he took the responsibility seriously enough to be nervous about it.

But I was also in my exclamation marveling at sponsorship itself as it is practiced in A.A. Under what other circumstances could one have envisaged this fellow behaving in this manner? Where else would he have found the *opportunity* to do so? Sponsorship is what made that conversation and all that it represents possible. That night, too, noting how much Vito cared about his sponsee, I was struck by the strange fact that at times we desire good for another more than we do for ourselves. And that this desire itself ends up doing us good by bringing out the best in ourselves. I did not express it to myself in this way then, but the thought reveals yet another facet of Bill W.'s insight into what I am calling reciprocity.

It is not surprising that this should be the case. Like meetings, sponsorship began with that first encounter between Bill and Dr. Bob, arising as it did out of their common need, their coming together on the common ground of the disease they suffered from, and their somehow being helped by helping—sponsoring—each other. And it has been practiced that way ever since, in a rather informal way, according to the needs, capabilities, and desires of both parties. There are no rules to be observed, either in sponsoring or in being sponsored. "The Big Book" and "The Twelve and Twelve" only allude to sponsorship, they don't discuss it. In keeping with A.A.'s thoroughgoing respect for individual freedom, the brief A.A. pamphlet devoted to the topic makes suggestions based on what people have found to be helpful over the years; it does not prescribe.

So how did my young thug come to be Andy's sponsor? Andy asked him to be, that's how. From the very beginning, every A.A. member is advised to get a sponsor, even a temporary one, someone to provide constant, close support, especially in the early days of sobriety. The choice of sponsor is left up to the sponsee. In order to avoid any romantic entanglement in the relationship at a time when they are so emotionally vulnerable, beginners are usually advised to choose a sponsor of the same sex. (Gays and lesbians, or anyone else for that matter, may choose a sponsor of the opposite sex.) The prospective sponsor is free, as Vito was, to take on the responsibility of sponsorship, or, for good reason, to decline it.

Any sober member of A.A. can sponsor someone. There are no courses to be taken to qualify, no credentials required, no category of certified sponsors. Sponsors learn what they need to know the way everything is learned in A.A.—from their own experience of having been sponsored, from listening at meetings to what others have to say about sponsorship, from the gleanings in A.A. literature. This makes what may at first seem a daunting charge quite manageable, as I realized when I became a sponsor myself. The sponsor doesn't need special gifts, or insight, or training. The sponsor only has to pass on what was passed on to him or her. By now we could expect—hope—that someone has asked Andy to sponsor him. And so it goes, illustrating another principle of Alcoholics Anonymous—the thoroughgoing egalitarianism in assuming responsibility for A.A.'s mission. There are no hierarchies, aristocracies, or meritocracies here.

The main task of sponsors, especially in the early days of sobriety, is to help beginners stay away from a drink "a day at a time." This is done chiefly by introducing them to the A.A. program and to other A.A. members, by encouraging them to attend meetings and providing transportation for them, if necessary, by sharing the wisdom gained from their own experience. Many sponsors ask beginners to call them every day. The daily call, a tender of commitment on the part of the sponsee, establishes some order and discipline in what are often chaotic lives, and signals the beginning of the end of the isolation that many suffer from. It provides both with a way of getting to know the other. As the relationship develops, the daily conversation gives the sponsee the opportunity to bring up other concerns and problems, and there are usually many in the wreckage of an alcoholic past. The sponsor is the one with whom one talks about matters too personal or painful to bring up at a meeting. Confidentiality is assured.

The sponsor is consulted, too, about decisions to be made and she will advise, in accord with A.A. practice, that no major decisions, especially in the area of romance, be made during the first year of sobriety. Is there any more hackneyed excuse for drinking than a broken heart? Is anyone less capable of entering into a healthy relationship than the newly sober person with nerves still raw, judgment still cloudy, emotions as unstable as any adolescent's?

I chose as my sponsor a woman who was to all appearances not very much like me. Cassandra is a wife and mother, not a working woman, not a Roman Catholic. Of Greek descent, and rather dramatic looking with a white streak running up the middle of her black hair, she seemed to me both earthy and wise, spiritual in a sensible way. She did not suggest that I call her every day, but we spoke often. She introduced me to A.A. etiquette—to thank the speaker after a meeting, to pass and not speak if I had come in late, to help with putting away the chairs after a meeting. I learned from her about respecting the anonymity of others, and not gossiping about what we hear at meetings.

Like some others from whom the compulsion to drink is lifted at their first meeting, I, gratefully, had no desire for alcohol since my stay in the rehab. (Except for crediting this blessing to the grace of God, we can't explain it to each other, so please don't expect me to explain it to you.) But I suffered acutely from what we call "stinking thinking." My sponsor listened patiently to my complaints, the ups and downs—mostly downs—in my relationships, to my feelings of anger, frustration, and failure. I found her quick to understand and sympathize. Mostly, as I recall, she did not give me advice, which I probably could not have heard anyway. She knew, as I came to know in the program, that many of my problems would be resolved as my nervous system adjusted to a life without the sedative of alcohol, and as I began to change "under the influence" of A.A.

Cassandra encouraged and commiserated with me as, in the next few years, I looked for employment. We nuns are always assured of the necessities of life, but those of us who can make a financial contribution to the community are expected to do so. And since my religious community no longer assigned us to ministries in our own institutions, as in pre–Vatican II days, but allowed us "choice of ministry," I needed to find a position that suited me. I did some teaching, was hired by a religious publisher that went out of business within a year, served a short and troubled stint as an assistant to the superior in one of our communities. I finally found gratifying work with an interreligious magazine. A decade later, feeling the need for more solitude and after taking counsel with Cassandra, I received permission from my religious superior to live alone, and moved into a two-room flat not far from the convent where I had been living. The solitude proved to be especially beneficial when I took up writing full time several years ago.

When the sponsor judges the time is right, she will put the beginner on the steps and guide her through them. Most often the sponsor is the person to whom we admit "the exact nature of our wrongs" in the Fifth Step. She is the one who goes over the "list of all persons we had harmed" in the Eighth Step, exercising her judgment as to whether an amends is called for; in our extravagant egoism some alcoholics imagine they owe the world an apology. It is in these ways that the sponsor functions as a spiritual guide, something like a spiritual director, with an important difference. She need not keep the boundaries between client and director usually observed by professionals. She is, in fact, encouraged by A.A. literature to speak freely about herself and her life, before, during, and after drinking; about her failures and character defects; about how she did the steps, and what benefits she has derived from them.

As the years passed my relationship with my sponsor deepened and changed, and in full accord with A.A.'s principles of mutuality, Cassandra confided to me her fear for and anguish over a mentally ill, sometimes suicidal, son (who has, thank God, since achieved a healthy degree of stability). I prayed for both of them, the least that I could do. She was comforted by my nun's prayers, as people are, though they are by reason of my being a nun no more effective than anyone else's. My problems began to seem small by comparison with hers, and I was humbled by her enduring faith in this years-long travail.

Then women in the program began to ask me to sponsor them. In every case except one, my sponsees, for one reason or another, had lost or were changing sponsors; they were not beginners, which made my task easier in a way. But over the next several years, three of these women lost adult children, one to cancer, two to accidental drug overdose. I hope that I was able to be of some comfort to them. There is so little, really, that one can say or do for others in this tragic, most painful loss, which seems to go against the very laws of nature itself. I listened, especially to Elsa, who called me frequently, not until her grief abated—that takes years—but until she became weary of talking. And when, literally crazed with grief, she was obsessing over what she thought was a drug-related plot behind the death of her son, I was able to keep her from what might have been a dangerous course of action. So at a time when I was feeling quite useless in other areas of my life, sponsoring these women was at least as helpful to me as it was to them.

If a sponsee is not following the suggestions given—we don't order, we suggest (though pretty strongly, I must admit)—some sponsors "fire" her. I don't. I have never fired a sponsee. I have made by mutual agreement with a sponsee a decision to terminate the relationship. But I don't pursue a recalcitrant sponsee either. If she wants whatever I am able to give her, I am willing to try to help. But, ultimately, it is up to her.

A sponsee whom I had not heard from in years, Kathleen, began drinking again last year, not her first slip. Her youngest son, an A.A. member himself, called me one night, fearful that his mother, locked in her apartment, might do herself harm. He would get a locksmith to open the apartment door if I could come over. Because we are advised not to go alone on this kind of Twelfth-Step work, I immediately called an A.A. friend. Without a moment's hesitation she agreed to accompany me. Before the night was over, we had gotten Kathleen into a rehab at a nearby hospital. She has done her Fourth and Fifth Steps again, this time with me, is working on her Eighth Step, and celebrated her "first" anniversary this past October.

Several months after the anniversary, at my initiative and with me as leader, she and another woman I sponsor went out speaking, that is, we visited another group at which they were to be the guest speakers. I sensed that Kathleen, who readily admits her alcoholism, had not yet *honestly* faced up to her past. She still seemed to me at that time to see herself as a victim, taking little responsibility for her part in the broken marriages, family estrangements, and financial disasters that were part of her story; she seemed to blame her drinking on the terrible things that she has suffered in her life. "The Big Book" places great emphasis on "the capacity to be honest," giving those who are "constitutionally incapable of grasping and developing a manner of living which demands rigorous honesty" a "less than average chance of recovery." It was my hope that this time-tested tool of the program—telling your story to others, *hearing* yourself tell your story—might bring this strong and extremely well-defended woman to a greater degree of honesty.

Well, I felt that my plan had not worked at all. Instead of taking up the half hour allotted to each speaker, she spoke for only ten minutes, and mostly about the last year. Even in such a short accounting, she mentioned past sufferings—family illnesses, the death of a son, the pain of which had led her to "sedate" herself with alcohol. I believe that she was in unspeakable pain then. After a brief moment of relief—maybe—drinking, with the terrible guilt, remorse, depression, and alienation of others that accompany it, only adds to the pain. And these consequences have their part in what Kathleen suffers now. Judging from my experience, however, the source of the pain lies deeper.

The remedy for her anguish, I believe, is that she face the truth, especially the truth about herself, however devastating it seems. She may feel, as I felt, that if she opens the floodgate of her sadness, the tears will never stop. But "the truth is our friend," as one of the nuns said to me a long time ago. It only becomes noxious when we bury it, when it lies inside, the source of a secretly tormenting ache. When we acknowledge it with the rigorous honesty that A.A. calls for, healing can begin—in ourselves, in the relationships with those we love, and with God. The Gospel says it: "The truth will make you free" (Jn. 8:32). It does.

That is what I believed at the time I was writing the first draft of this chapter as it appears above. And I still do believe it. But, as I have come to understand since, the truth that I was so concerned that Kathleen face was only half the story, half of the truth.

Here is what happened. Kathleen, in her own good time, began to make amends to the people whose names she had written down on her Eighth-Step list, as the Ninth Step suggests. She approached her oldest son, who is also in the program, and, in a strategy that she and I had agreed upon, asked *him* to tell *her* how she had harmed him. Instead, he reminded her of how good she had been to him in his lifetime—the scrapes she had gotten him out of when he was drinking, the money she had lent him, the jobs she helped him get. And he told her how proud and happy he was to see her sober now. She was overcome, could not talk to me about the encounter without tears. More surprisingly, the same kind of thing occurred when she visited a former spouse in a nursing home to make amends to him.

"Oh," I said to her then, "this is how God is dealing with you." I meant that God, kinder and wiser than I— as if that need be said—was enabling her to see all the goodness in herself, a much better "strategy" than mine, for sure. Now, without feeling an utter failure (which she has confided to me was the reason behind the ten-minute story; she felt that she had no message to carry), she is going forward with her Ninth Step. And I recognized at once, and again, my tendency to focus on the negative in others and in myself. The insight I have gained about myself and about God in all of this has in turn affected my prayer. I try to pray now not so conscious of faults and failings in myself and in others, even when I am asking for healing for them and for me. Rather, I place all of us in our goodness before God, try to appreciate and savor that goodness, and trust God to take care of the rest.

As it happened on the night of our speaking engagement. the second speaker, Eileen, was left to fill the rest of the hour She highlighted the part that denial, the bugaboo of the disease of alcoholism that tells you that you don't have a disease, played in her story. In fact, it was through sponsoring Eileen that I came to understand this phenomenon: *Don't Even kNow I Am Lying*, as another A.A. acronym has it.

My own denial about my alcoholism was short-lived; I began to worry about drinking compulsively very early on. After all, unlike many, whose work or social life condones or even encourages drinking, my professed way of life with its ideals of discipline, self-abnegation, and poverty was clearly at odds with drinking too much. So it was shame rather than denial that kept me from seeking help. But I had to deal with the latter when Eileen asked me to sponsor her.

She was the daughter of an alcoholic father, had become a daily drinker herself, was divorced from a heavy drinker, made an impetuous and disastrous second marriage, and, like all of us, had done and suffered hurtful things while under the influence of alcohol. One of her sons had preceded her into A.A., and she arrived at his first anniversary celebration tipsy. But none of this, nor her attendance at meetings for several years afterwards, had really convinced her that she was an alcoholic. Two plus two was there on the blackboard in great big numbers, but it just didn't add up to four for her. It made me crazy that I could not *make* her see it. I understood then that denial is not lying as we usually understand it, that is, knowing the truth and purposely distorting it or concealing it from others. The person in denial cannot see, or does not allow herself to see, what is really the case. (I think that we all engage in denial in one form or another. I know I do, especially in my relationship with God.) But until that veil was lifted from Eileen's eyes, she simply could not see the truth about her drinking or about other unhealthy dependencies in her life.

She acknowledged in telling her story that she went to meetings for years hoping to discover that she was not an alcoholic. But she kept coming to A.A. because she knew that I believed that she was. Finally, she realized that the reason she wanted to get out of the fellowship was precisely *so that* she could drink again. With that realization, her denial began to dissipate, freeing her to face, with a lot of help from a good therapist, other deep-seated problems. Far from finding her therapy at odds with the program or feeling that I am in competition with the therapist (A.A. encourages getting outside help when needed, I often ask Eileen what Audrey thinks of a given situation. It turns out that we almost always agree in our assessment and advice. And it has been a source of support for me, without any training in psychology as I am, to know that my counsel has the backing of a professional.

I was talking to one of the nuns, not in A.A., the same night that I was to meet these two women to go out speaking. Through a contact made by Marie, the nun, I had taken a mutual acquaintance who was just out of a rehab to her first meeting. She had not returned my subsequent call, and I promised Marie that I would call her again. When I said that I had to leave to meet my sponsees, Marie marveled, "What a ministry you have in A.A.!" "No," I answered, shaking my head and somewhat abruptly, "that's not it at all." I did not explain for lack of time. But I don't think of A.A. as a ministry in the way that we often use the word, with its connotation of serving those less fortunate than ourselves, admirable as that may be. This is just the way A.A. works. This is what people did, do, for me. If I can help any soul as wretched as I was to find the serenity I have found, I am happy to try, and I, in turn, am helped. On second thought, maybe that's how Christian ministry in the service of the gospel, the *good news,* is supposed to and does work at its best.

So a sponsor is teacher/learner, guide/fellow traveler, spiritual advisor/advisee, sometimes friend. After all these years, my sponsor is still only a phone call away if I need her. As we used to say about a wife, everyone (not only in A.A.) should have one. Ideally—not everyone gets asked—everyone should also have the opportunity to be a sponsor. It is an exquisite joy, when it happens, to witness the transformation that takes place as sponsees pass from misery to peace. It is a privilege to be a companion on that journey.

A Meditation on Grace
and the Promises

THE LAST PART OF THE section in "The Big Book" dealing with Steps Eight and Nine, familiarly known as "the Promises," begins like this:

If we are painstaking about this phase of our development, we will be amazed before we are half way through. We are going to know a new freedom and a new happiness. We will not regret the past nor wish to shut the door on it. We will comprehend the word serenity and we will know peace.

And the paragraph ends: "We will suddenly realize that God is doing for us what we could not do for ourselves." In Christian language, we are becoming aware of the grace of God in our lives, not experiencing it for the first time but becoming aware of it as grace. We are, in other words, passing from the purgative to the illuminative way.

I don't think that we hear enough about the grace of God these days. I am not sure that we ever did in the sermons we listened to in church. But the Baltimore Catechism of my youth and my later theological studies parsed this rich theological notion for me: sanctifying grace, "a sharing in the life of God Himself"; actual grace, "a divine impulse moving a person to perform acts above his natural powers"; the state of grace, my condition as a baptized Catholic unless I alienate myself from God in some fundamental way; and, reversing the phrase, the grace of state, the special assistance received to fulfill the responsibilities of one's vocation, state in life—as a parent, a nun, etc.

Underlying all the catechism questions and answers and the theological disquisitions about grace is the notion of God with us, within us, guiding us, helping us, empowering us. It is a lovely notion. Contrary to the Pelagianism condemned as a heresy in the fifth century, which credits our salvation and sanctification to our own efforts,

grace sees all as gift, freely given by God, unearned, unde-
served, by us.

Jesus captures the element of gift, working mysteri-
ously in our lives, independent of our efforts, in this
little parable in Mark 4, one of my favorites.

> The kingdom of God is as if someone would
> scatter seed on the ground, and would sleep
> and rise night and day, and the seed would
> sprout and grow, he does not know how. The
> earth produces of itself, first the stalk, then the
> head, then the full grain in the head. But when
> the grain is ripe, he goes in with his sickle,
> because the harvest has come.

The parable may also imply something of the elusiveness
of the reality of grace, or, more accurately, of our failure
to recognize it as it occurs in our lives. We do not see it
happening, don't see the plant growing; we are "asleep"
most of the time.

In a short essay entitled "Reflections on the Experience of Grace," Karl Rahner, the great twentieth-century
German Jesuit theologian, asks if we think we have actually experienced grace, whether "it is possible to experience grace in this life." Then in a series of questions, he
"tentatively and cautiously" directs us to what he believes

are signs of grace, or "the spirit," in our experience. Contrary to what we might expect, Rahner's questions are not about what we usually think of as the supernatural—strange occurrences, dramatic events, or high states of mystical prayer. He asks:

> Have we ever kept quiet, even though we wanted to defend ourselves when we had been unfairly treated? Have we ever forgiven someone even though we got no thanks for it and our silent forgiveness was taken for granted? . . . Have we ever sacrificed something without receiving any thanks or recognition for it, and even without a feeling of inner satisfaction?

He concludes that if we have had such experiences we have experienced grace. We have experienced that "the spirit is more than merely a part of this temporal world, that our "meaning is not exhausted by the meaning and fortune of this world . . . or taken from the success of this world." Such acts, neither understood nor rewarded now, point to something beyond time. They point to the eternal.

At my A.A. meetings, the slogan "There but for the grace of God go I" is displayed at the front of the room on a plaque. The plaque reminds us of the initial blessing we received in being enabled to stop drinking. And it is, theologically speaking, properly called grace, because it was beyond our power, inexplicable, sometimes even to ourselves. Why, one day, just like every other day with its dreary routine of getting, hiding, drinking alcohol, did Mary decide to call her uncle in A.A. and go with him to her first meeting? She doesn't know, even after eighteen years in the program. But other than in this saying, in my experience of A.A., the word "grace" is not used.

It is, however, understood and talked about. In statements reminiscent of Fehner's questions, the Promises continue:

> No matter how far down the scale we have gone, we will see how our experience can benefit others. That feeling of uselessness and self-pity will disappear. We will lose interest in selfish things and gain interest in our fellows. Self-seeking will slip away. Our whole attitude and outlook upon life will change. Fear of people and of economic insecurity will leave us. We will intuitively know how to handle situations which used to baffle us.

Perhaps it is because the Promises describe a way of life so at odds with our past that we are aware of them as blessings, as grace, beyond our own power, and hence are aware of their source. It is the awareness that is crucial. Awareness—of God's presence in the Christian and Jewish traditions, known as awakening, enlightenment, wisdom in others—is the goal of many of the spiritual practices of the great world religions.

According to Christian belief, if we had eyes [the awareness] to see, we would know that the world, created by God, sanctified by the incarnation of Jesus Christ, redeemed by his blood, and filled with God's spirit, is permeated, drenched, charged with the grace of God. It is all around us, within us. The poet Gerard Manley Hopkins speaks of "the dearest freshness deep down things." Harder to see and believe in, I think, is the dearest freshness deep down people—hardest, perhaps, to see in ourselves—all made in the image of God, however much that image has been distorted, profaned, disfigured.

Well, in A.A. I can see that image emerge, can see the faces of people change from tortured to serene, from bleary-eyed and blotchy and flushed to clear and healthy. And I can hear people as they speak in meetings change from bitter, angry, resentful, whining, and negative, as I was when I came in, to people of peace and humility and gratitude.

I think of Casey, an erstwhile neer-do-well, an unemployed, unemployable con man, who arranged to spend most winters in the penitentiary (he always gives the word six syllables—pen-i-ten-ti-a-ry) where he was assured of a warm bed and "three squares a day." Last month he told that in one of his several unsuccessful attempts at A.A., still a bamboozler, he had actually asked an A.A. member, if he, Casey, could copy the other guy's Fourth Step: "Made a searching and fearless inventory of ourselves"!

Of Irish descent, like many A.A.s in my part of the country, besides having inherited the curse of the drink, Casey also has the gift of eloquence. At one anniversary celebration of his sobriety in A.A., he spoke of the date of his last drink as his birthday, when he was given a new life. As his Fourth of July, when he became a free man. As his Thanksgiving. And his Christmas, when he came to know himself as a son of God. That anniversary had to be seven or eight years ago. I still remember what Casey said. He is still here. And so am I. By the grace of God.

The Promises conclude: "Are these extravagant promises? We think not. They are being fulfilled among us—sometimes quickly, sometimes slowly. They will always materialize if we work for them." Jesus' parable, too, making its point in the exaggerated and selective way of parables, leaves out all the hard work the farmer has to do—the ploughing, preparing the soil, planting, weeding—"doing the footwork," as we say. Faith and works, grace and free will—that mysterious mix, that alternating rhythm. But whence comes faith, and who enables us to work? Finally, it is all grace.

Entering on the
Illuminative Way

AT THE END OF STEP TEN, "The Big Book" says: "To some extent we have become God-conscious. We have begun to develop this vital sixth sense." Before we move to Step Eleven, "Sought through prayer and meditation to improve our conscious contact with God," always as we understand Him, "praying only for knowledge of His will for us and the power to carry that out," we have to ask about *how* we have become God-conscious, and *what* God it is that we have already begun to know and love. What God is it that we now seek to encounter in prayer and meditation, in the illuminative way, the stage of "growth in the knowledge and love of God within a contemplative experience," as *The Encyclopedia of Catholicism* describes it?

Susan has been in the program for about two years. At the Sunday night women's meetings we have learned of the painful and difficult decision she made this year to separate from her husband. We also know of the anguish she has experienced in dealing with her adolescent daughter's temptations to suicide.

On the Sunday before Thanksgiving, quietly weeping, Susan told us this story. Feeling no enmity toward her husband and wanting to preserve a sense of family, especially for her daughter's sake, she invited him to dinner. Her daughter had just returned from a weekend spent with her confirmation class. At one session during the weekend, the boys and girls were divided into discussion groups, and Susan's daughter—no doubt, Susan said, because her rabbi knew of her problem—was assigned to the group that was discussing suicide. At dinner she told her parents how she had struggled over whether to talk about herself in the group. She did. And she and her parents were then able to talk calmly together about this terrible affliction.

I don't pretend to know all the mingled emotions that Susan's gentle tears expressed. I sensed that they

were tears of sorrow, regret, pain, but mostly of gratitude. No glib and easy gratitude, but born of a small,
precious mercy found in the midst of suffering.

"My name is ____ and I am a grateful alcoholic." I
hear this often. Some go on to clarify that they are not
grateful to be alcoholics—no one is initially—but they
are grateful for the program. Others go a step further.
They are convinced that without their alcoholism and
A.A. they never would have found the way of life they
now cherish. Gratitude is frequently the theme suggested
by the leader at topic meetings. Sponsors advise making a
gratitude list when one is in a slump or "on the pity pot."

A winsome virtue, containing elements of humility
and unselfishness, gratitude directs our attention away
from all that our needy, demanding egos see that we
don't have to all that we do have, and mostly don't
deserve. It recognizes gifts as gifts (or grace as grace) and
goes looking for someone to be grateful to. Thus I deem
it a virtue that puts us on the path to the illuminative
way. Gratitude leads us to a generous and caring God.
And this God is a God we can love.

I was not capable of gratitude when I was buried in
the tangled, painful, self-enclosed emotions of early
sobriety. When that dark world is the only world you
know, what is there to be grateful for? I was relieved not

to be drinking, but relief, as I came to understand, is not gratitude. Relief descends upon the self and remains there. It is directionless.

The fact is that I didn't realize how sick I was until I began to get better. Little by little, I came to know some peace, first of all, you may remember, at A.A. meetings. Relief gave way to gratitude, to my group, just for being there, and to A.A. as a whole, just for existing. As some of the choking negative feelings and attitudes were uprooted from my heart in the steps, many of which are explicitly pointed toward God, like most in A.A., I became grateful to God for the degree of freedom and serenity I experienced.

You may think that because I am a nun the order would have been reversed for me, God first, others second. (Don't forget that I was a sick nun whose spirit was dead.) The truth of the matter is that my sure *experience* of having been gratefully saved in A.A. did lead me to a greater knowledge and love of God. Then I began to wonder how I as a Christian experience salvation from sin, to wonder how grateful I am for *that,* and more specifically, how I experience Jesus as my savior, as the one whose salvific life, death, and resurrection reveal God's love to me, as I claim to believe. I am going to try to answer these questions later.

But the questions of how we come to know and love God in A.A., what God it is that we come to know and love, even when that God is the God of our own understanding, are crucial here. I believe the answers to those questions, as I have found them, revolve around the elements of experience, story, and fellowship, the word A.A. uses for community.

The experience that brought me to A.A. was that of being wretchedly unhappy and unable to help myself. That was the raw experience. Experience, however, begs for understanding, interpretation. I came to understand that I was sick, was suffering from a physical, mental, and spiritual disease. And that the remedy for it was to be found in A.A. I was taught this not by way of medical diagnosis, or from reading technical descriptions of the disease, or from lengthy discussion of its symptoms and "cure," but from stories. There is no abstraction in stories. You cannot get any closer to experience than stories. When people told their stories at meetings—what they were like, what happened to them, and how they had changed in A.A.—I recognized myself in them. Their stories and those I read in "The Big Book" gave me hope.

Three hundred and ninety out of the 561 pages in "The Big Book" are given over to stories, short stories with titles like "Rum, Radio, and Rebellion," "Me an Alcoholic?" "Belle of the Bar." I used to read them when, no longer sedated by alcohol, I couldn't sleep at night. The more desperate and sordid the story, the greater the comfort it gave me. If these people could become sober, so could I.

Neither the stories I heard in person nor those that I read engaged in any discussion of "the nature of God." Like good fiction, except, of course, that they were true, they do not tell, they show: I was sick and I am recovering; I was miserable and I am happy; I was lonely and I have found fellowship; I felt useless and now there is purpose and meaning in my life. "I once was lost, and now am found. . . ." How can I not be grateful for this "amazing grace"?

To whom shall I be grateful? A.A.—"it's a spiritual program," we say—sends us looking for God. And the God that gratitude finds is a powerful God, who desires our well-being, who can and will help us if we ask, who has in fact helped us and helps us still. By virtue of our own experience and the stories we hear from others, then, this God cannot be the stern lawgiver, the punishing God that many say they were taught to believe in. This God has to be a loving God, whose love for us invites love in return. I don't know that I have ever heard the phrase "the love of God" meaning either God's love for us or ours for God in A.A. That language simply is not used. But it is always implied.

Life, however, is not always sweet. God's love does not always come to us clothed in good health, good jobs, good luck. I am struck, in fact, by how often people fairly new to A.A. seem to be visited by suffering, illness, misfortune, the death of a loved one. After three years in the program, Meg, in a fairly short period of time, had a mastectomy, lost her father, went through hell with a teenager on drugs. She was not grateful for these tribulations. She was grateful that she found the strength in the fellowship and in her faith to endure them. And she knew—she *knew*—that if she had still been drinking, everything would have been not easier to go through but incomparably harder and that her drinking itself would have made things worse. She was sober at her father's funeral. She had her own experience in A.A. on which to draw in knowing when to step in and confront her son and when "to let go and let God." Other women in the program who have had mastectomies supported her.

And she had her faith. She is a Catholic. She unabashedly tells us that she prays only to Our Lady, who embodies for her the goodness and kindness of God. She may not know and might not care if she did know that some Christian feminist and liberation theologians are making just that claim for Mary. She has found the God of her understanding.

Yet even in the absence of misfortune, and even when grateful to God for blessings in the good times and strength in bad times, I don't think that it is *easy* to believe that God *loves* us, that God loves *me*. I have heard it, the statement "God loves you," all my life. Preachers preach it, more now perhaps than in the past. Theologians commonly discuss the topic of the love of God. All of this may illumine and support the conviction that one is loved, but neither preaching nor teaching can create it. The obstacle, I suspect, in coming to this radical, root, belief is that we don't easily love ourselves.

I came to this conclusion, again in A.A., from the observation of its opposite—namely, that people who talked about hating God seemed to hate themselves. I myself at one time had been filled with that awful feeling of self-loathing. I never would have said that I hated God, but neither did I have any sense at all that God loved me. It was only when I had the experience of being loved, when I had the experience of being lovable, that I began to be able to love myself.

"Let us love you until you can love yourself"—another A.A. saying. Does it sound maudlin? It was given teeth for me in the statement of one man who used it in contrast to the message he was given in his family: "Let us hate you until you hate yourself." In A.A., we find acceptance from people who honestly admit to being just like us in all our frailty. We are carefully listened to. We are thought worth saving, and people like our sponsors and friends give us their time, their attention, their energy. No matter how many times we may fail at becoming sober, we are never kicked out, never "excommunicated" for that or anything else, since the *only* requirement for membership in A.A. is a *desire* to stop drinking. Then, as we become sober ourselves, we are enabled, and we want, to act in these ways toward others.

Think about my young thug. Surely gratitude for what he had received in the fellowship made him want to pass the gift on to others. Gratitude begets generosity. "You received without payment; give without payment" (Mt. 10:8), as the Christian scriptures say. And surely he found himself more lovable as a sponsor trying to help his buddy than he did in the life he was living before A.A. Perhaps these sentiments brought him to a greater knowledge and love of God and to a belief in God's love for him; I don't know. I suspect, however, that he had a better chance of coming to such beliefs in A.A. than in some of our religious institutions. "The medium is the message," said media pundit Marshall McLuhan decades ago. In A.A, the medium of acceptance, caring, and respect for individual freedom doesn't get mixed up with any other messages than that of love.

I believe that most of us do not come to know God's love for us until we love ourselves. I believe that most human beings cannot come to love themselves alone. For that we need fellowship—community—a community of equals in which we are both givers and receivers. Is this another instance of the deep reciprocity that is part of our nature? Did Bill Wilson intuit this, too, in discovering that he couldn't stay sober alone?

So experience, stories, and community. And running through all of them as the life-giving nutrient that brings us to the light, gratitude.

The Illuminative Way, "Sought Through Prayer and Meditation"

The Eleventh Step

I TUMBLE OUT OF BED when the alarm goes off, directly onto my knees, my feet not even touching the floor first. I thank God for a good night's sleep, if I had one, murmur a brief prayer not to drink today. Even though the thought of taking a drink doesn't cross my mind, I do not want to take the gift of my sobriety for granted. Complacency is as much an enemy in sobriety as it is in the spiritual life, and I have heard too many stories of people relapsing after ten, twelve, fifteen years to want to put myself in that position. I pray also, maybe a bit more fervently, for help with my writing today.

After a shower and breakfast, I sit on the couch in my living room/bedroom for my morning prayer and meditation. Today the autumn sun, low in the sky, finds its way through the blinds, making a delicate latticed pattern on the wall that I face. It prompts me to be grateful for the sun, and then for the beauty and beneficence of all creation.

I read the entry for November 23rd from the little meditation book *A Day at a Time*. It reminds me not to give in to "the old urge to control everything and everybody," not to try to be "the actor who insisted on writing the script, producing, directing . . . running the whole show . . . forever trying to arrange and rearrange the lights, lines, set (that's me!), and most of all, the other players' performances." I read the scriptures for the day from my missalette, both apocalyptic—Daniel interpreting Nebuchadnezzar's dream, Jesus describing the endtime. We are approaching the liturgical season of Advent.

Then I name those for whom I wish to pray—just name them. Kay undergoing further tests for cancer. Jean, a college classmate who is on dialysis, and her troubled son Ted. My family. My community. My church. My country.

I settle into my meditation. Nothing from the scriptures today catches my attention. I reflect instead on a favorite Gospel passage: Jesus going off alone at night to pray. How did he pray? What did he think, feel? I do not intend to intrude. I respect his desire to be alone. What does it mean to be alone with God?

After about half an hour, I say the Third and Seventh Step prayers as they are found in "The Big Book":

God, I offer myself to Thee—to build with me and do with me as Thou wilt. Relieve me of the bondage of self, that I may better do Thy will. Take away my difficulties, that victory over them may bear witness to those I would help of Thy power, Thy love, and Thy way of life. May I do Thy will always.

and

My Creator, I am now willing that you should have all of me, good and bad. I pray that you now remove from me every single defect of character which stands in the way of my usefulness to you and my fellows. Grant me strength, as I go out from here to do your bidding. Amen.

I like both of these prayers for the way they direct personal concerns and the virtuous life toward the service of others—"to build with me," "to bear witness to those I would help," "that stands in the way of my usefulness"—the touchstone in my book of any genuine spirituality. The petition "Relieve me of the bondage of self" sums the matter up.

I have always liked the phrase "all of me, good and bad," too. It curbs my tendency to want to clean up my act before presenting myself to God, like the housewife who tidies up the house before the cleaning woman comes. Recently, a young woman in the program gave me another angle on the phrase. Since it was precisely what Helen thought were her good points that got her in trouble, she said, she doesn't trust her own self-assessment any more. She simply offers her whole being to God and leaves it to God to separate the wheat from the chaff. And until I heard Jane confess it, I had thought that I was the only one who found the loophole in the phrase "which stands in the way of my usefulness to you and to others." Surely, this dear little vice doesn't hurt anyone. . . .

I conclude by saying in Italian this prayer ascribed to St. Francis. I don't speak Italian, but I know enough Latin to make it out. The straightforward and insistent *"Dammi"* satisfies me more than its timid-sounding English equivalent "Give me," or the more formal "Grant me."

O alto e glorioso Dio, illumina le tenebre del cuore mio. Dammi una fede retta, speranza certa, carità perfetta, e umiltà profonda. Dammi, Signore, senno e discernimento per compiere la tua vera e santa volontà. Amen.

(O great and glorious God, illumine the shadows of my heart. Give me a true faith, firm hope, perfect love, and deep humility. Give me, O Lord, the wisdom and right judgment to fulfill your true and holy will.)

I go about my day's work, writing, doing chores, preparing and eating lunch and dinner. I say grace before them. I don't pray much or very consciously during the day. The startlingly yellow leaves against the blue sky as I drive up the beach road wrings a little prayer from me. As does the creek water lying deep, if it's high tide against the tawny rushes of the marsh. I don't seem to pray if it is low tide and not beautiful.

In the late afternoon or early evening, I say the rosary. I light a little candle before the framed reproduction of Rublev's mysterious and imponderably beautiful painting of the Trinity. It hangs above several icons of Jesus and Mary and a holy card of Giotto's St. Francis that rest on the radiator cover in my entranceway. I walk slowly back and forth in my two-room flat, or outside, if the weather is nice. I alternate between lingering over the words of the prayers—"thy kingdom come," "full of grace," "pray for us sinners," and the mysteries of the rosary—joyful, sorrowful, glorious, depending on the day of the week. Joyful: a bittersweet joy, Simeon telling Mary that because of her child a sword will pierce her heart, just as every mother's heart will be pierced by her child in some way. Sorrowful: Jesus in blood-sweating fear and mental anguish on the Mount of Olives. Glorious: the Spirit descending upon the apostles, as the Spirit hovered over the waters in a fecund embrace at the creation, and as now over the bay that I can see from my front door. The rosary takes me about twenty-five minutes.

Before I go to bed, I kneel again. I do a quick Tenth Step, an inventory of actions and attitudes during the day. If it has been an unproductive day for writing, I might not even have what Anne Lamott calls "a shitty first draft" to show for the day's work. Then I'm especially grateful that Jenny, for whom I am a kind of backup sponsor, called, as she does almost daily. We plan her day together. And I have at least that to offer to God, even as I am aware that I'm still trying to show God that I am "a good girl."

"Make me a good girl" was part of the prayer I said when I was growing up. "God bless Mommy and Daddy, and Betsy, and Granny and Grampa, and all my aunts and uncles. . . . Make me a good girl. . . . And thank-

you for making my toe better," the last said in the ever-
accumulating prayer long after whichever toe was healed
of whatever injury it had suffered. It comes right out of
my mouth now once I start the prayer going. I said this
prayer on my knees at night beside my bed. As a cradle
Catholic, I was accustomed to kneeling both in church
and at home, didn't give doing it a moment's thought.

Apparently many sponsors suggest that their sponsees kneel in the morning to ask for help in staying away
from a drink, and at night to say thank-you. "Hitting my
knees," the young guys call it. I understand that for those
of other faiths, Jews, for instance, the gesture may seem
too Christian, alien to them and their traditions. Others
seem to imply, however, that the posture itself, not its
associations, causes them difficulty. I began to realize that
kneeling had meaning for them, signified, I guessed, the
humble surrender they could not quite yet bring themselves to make.

I had stopped kneeling for private prayer in my "liberated" phase after Vatican II, when I and other nuns freed
ourselves from myriad rules, regulations, and customs,
many of them outdated or silly. But I kneel now. The realization that kneeling can and should express something—
powerlessness, surrender, humility—has brought me back
to the practice. There is a big difference, I have learned,
between rules and regulations and devotional practices,

at least when the practices are done mindfully and not just out of habit or in compliance with a law imposed by some outside authority.

Gone, too, from my spiritual repertoire during those liberated days was the twice-daily examen—an examination of conscience—made, according to the rule of my community, at noon and at night prayer. Ed, a Marlboro-looking man, balding and with a fine mustache, led a Tenth-Step meeting I attended. He spoke simply and strongly about how much he needed to continue "to take personal inventory," and shared with us the little list he uses for it every night. I asked him for a copy of the list. I began doing the Tenth Step.

And I had stopped praying the rosary too. It went out of fashion, as it were, in the intellectual circles in which I traveled. I am not sure that A.A. had anything to do with my taking it up again. Perhaps the down-to-earth, real-life, nontheoretical, storylike nature of the mysteries—pregnancy (the annunciation), birth (the nativity), the lost child (finding Jesus in the temple); Jesus' emotional, physical, and spiritual suffering in his passion and death; the promise of new life (the resurrection, the ascension)—maybe these had more meaning for me in my experience as a recovering alcoholic, sharing the lives of other recovering alcoholics.

But why, you may be asking, did it take these faithful A.A.s to bring me back to these practices? Don't we nuns often talk honestly and openly about these matters? Well, no, not in my experience, and for different and complex reasons. As young nuns we were forbidden to talk to anyone but the superior about our prayer, an example of the hierarchical control to which our entire lives were subject. Later—as they do now—some nuns began to meet not to talk about their prayer but to pray together. They read a passage from scripture, silently reflect on it, and then either address God vocally in prayer or share their thoughts about the passage. It seems to work well for them. I never quite got the hang of it. It felt artificial to me; you had to give God an awful lot of background information for your prayer to make sense to others. "O God, You know that I am going to an important meeting tomorrow. . . ." And I was too self-conscious. The temptation to put my best face forward, especially with people I lived with, was too strong.

When Sally told us at an A.A. meeting that she fled to the bathroom at work to get down on her knees to ask for help in a difficult situation the last thing on her mind was flaunting her prayerful self or giving us what in Catholic jargon is called "good example." She was sharing her weakness with us and telling us how she overcame it.

With some years of sobriety behind her, she wasn't tempted to drink. But the subtext of all that is shared at meetings is that all-too-real, concrete drink, which symbolizes our powerlessness in so many other ways. (I have not yet been able to figure out what might serve in the same way for me and my sisters. I suspect it might be our very real and concrete sinfulness—more on this later—but in a way of life geared to the attainment of perfection, we don't talk much about that either.)

So Sally wasn't trying to impress us or teach us. It is, however, because of what I have learned from people like her that before a committee meeting with the nuns last week, I asked for help in remaining calm when dealing with what I thought could be a sticky problem. (I did.) And that driving up to visit my family for Thanksgiving, I asked for the grace not to be critical or negative. (I wasn't.) I don't use the famous Serenity Prayer very much, but beginners, especially, say they repeat it, like a mantra, a hundred times a day. I believe them.

In the chapter on the Eleventh Step—"Sought through prayer and meditation to improve our conscious contact with God, *as we understood Him,* praying only for knowledge of His will for us and the power to carry that out"—"The Twelve and Twelve" directs us to consult the great body of literature on prayer and meditation from our own traditions and from others, where "a treasure trove for all seekers" is to be found. Prayer and meditation, the book claims, are as necessary for the life of the spirit as fresh air, food, and sunlight are for the body; "meditation is our step out into the sun" (the illuminative way).

If we think of prayer as talking to God, with or without words, our own or those of others, then we can think of meditation as listening to God—an attitude of open, silent receptiveness. It is more difficult to do and more difficult to talk about. "The Twelve and Twelve" offers the so-called Prayer of St. Francis as matter for meditation. Following the natural imagery ("fresh air," "sunlight"), the book suggests that we imagine ourselves on a sunlit beach, relaxed, and breathing deeply as we slowly read and reread the prayer, savoring its beauty and the beauty of our imaginary scene. We then try with our focused, constructive imaginations to get to the inner essence of the prayer, the self-forgetting sought for by Francis. Using our imaginations this way, the book says, "helps us to envision our spiritual objective before we try to move toward it."

A good number of A.A.s confess that they are not able to meditate in these ways. They describe listening at meetings as their meditation. That is where they are quiet, centered, but not self-centered. That is where they hear "God speaking to them through other people." Who is to say that they are wrong?

On the subject of prayer understood as petition, while we are always encouraged to ask for God's help, "The Twelve and Twelve" counsels to us to be careful in praying for specific things or outcomes for ourselves or for others, advising that we add the phrase "if it be Thy will" to such requests. It warns us against conceit in "asking God to do [things] *our* way" and in making "self-serving demand[s] of God for replies." It points out that claims of having had God's guidance on matters great and small may often be "well-intentioned unconscious rationalizations," and with rather rueful humor describes how disconcerting it can be to deal with the person who makes such claims. With the understanding of qualifications like these, the wisdom in the conclusion of the Eleventh Step, "praying only for knowledge of His will for us and the power to carry that out," is more apparent; the step doesn't seem to be presenting such an unrealistic and unattainable ideal.

Many of us, Catholics anyway, tend to use the phrase "God's will" only for dire events like illness, death, accidents, or when something difficult is asked of us. Even if that is all that the phrase meant, praying for God's power to endure what life brings assures us that we are not alone, ever, in anything that we have to face. Such a hard lesson to learn. I prefer, however, to think of God's will not as a test to be met, or a set of laws to be obeyed, but as God's dream for us, for who we might become and be. For me, that puts everything in perspective, the perspective of faith in a God who loves us.

Near the end of the chapter on the Eleventh Step, "The Twelve and Twelve" offers this sound and kind advice for those times when prayer is difficult or impossible, times of "dryness" or "desolation" in the Christian lexicon. Obviously written out of experience, it says:

> All of us, without exception, pass through times when we can pray only with the greatest exertion of will. . . . We are seized with a rebellion so sickening that we simply won't pray. When these things happen we should not think too ill of ourselves. We should simply resume prayer as soon as we can, doing what we know to be good for us.

Now stop for a moment, please. Think from whom all this solid advice on prayer and meditation is coming. Not from some sage or saint, but from Bill Wilson, a recovering alcoholic (though his name does not appear on the title page of either *Alcoholics Anonymous* or *Twelve*

Steps and Twelve Traditions). Think to whom it is directed. Not to a group whose life plan it was to dedicate themselves to prayer and good works, but to people who confess to having been self-willed, deluded, sick. That a life of prayer, not the occasional "foxhole prayer," is one of the conditions of lasting sobriety and serenity is surely as strange and as revealing as Bill W.'s realization in the hotel lobby in Akron. Revealing, that is, about all of us, about the human condition and the way of prayer and meditation as the way to peace and freedom and service.

Entering on the Unitive Way

A Meditation on Anonymity

I TUNED IN TO THE MID-
dle of National Public Radio's *All Things Considered*
some time about two months ago. A woman jazz singer
was being interviewed I didn't catch her name. Amidst
the usual questions about her music, her rise to promi-
nence in the world of jazz, came this unusual question,
or at least, a question unusually phrased. The interviewer
asked, "And you're a friend of Bill Wilson, aren't you?"
There was a pause. Then the singer said yes. Another
pause. Sensing something amiss, the interviewer jumped
into the silence. "For those of our listeners who don't

know, 'friends of Bill Wilson' is what members of Alco-holics Anonymous call themselves." The singer then picked up the beat and began to talk, not about A.A. but about her alcoholism, how it affected her life and her career. What was going on here?

The singer, as is her right if she so chooses, spoke openly of her struggle and suffering as an alcoholic. Even though that is what the interviewer probably intended by his question, she was taken aback for a moment. The question seemed to be asking about Alcoholics Anony-mous. And she dodged it. She was observing the Eleventh Tradition of A.A., which says that "our public relations policy is based on attraction rather than promo-tion; we need always maintain personal anonymity at the level of press, radio, and films." That is, as "The Twelve and Twelve" explains, "our names and pictures *as A.A. members* [italics mine] ought not to be broadcast, filmed, or publicly printed."

If you are not a member of A.A., this might seem unusual to you. Why confess that your life was a mess because of alcohol and not report about your recovery in A.A.? More to the point, why not spread the good news about A.A. in an effort to help other alcoholics? If you think about it for a moment, however, you will realize that you have rarely seen or heard, except in an oblique reference, an endorsement for A.A. from any public personage—Betty Ford. Liz Taylor, various stars of stage or screen—even when that person spoke openly about his or her alcoholism. You have never seen an ad for A.A., still less one like, say, Sarah Ferguson's for Weight Watchers, with a celebrity touting the benefits of the program. Have you ever wondered why? Probably not. I never did

Everybody easily understands one meaning of anonymous in the name Alcoholics Anonymous. They rightly understand it to mean that one never reveals the membership of another in the fellowship without permission. "What you see here, what you hear here, remains here" is announced at the beginning of open meetings in my group, mostly for the benefit of outsiders at those meetings. Members also maintain discretionary anonymity about themselves in order to safeguard their reputations, jobs, and privacy against the stigma that accompanies the disease. The Eleventh Tradition supports this. But it calls for more.

Like the other traditions, it was not set down beforehand as a blueprint for some ideal society. "The Twelve and Twelve" describes some of the "many painful experiences" that compelled the founders of A.A. to recognize that 'being in the public eye is hazardous, especially for us . . . people who by temperament are irrepressible promoters . . . that personal ambition has no place in A.A. . . . . If even one publicly got drunk, or was lured into using A.A.'s name for his own purposes, the damage might be irreparable." In order for A.A.'s mission to be effective, members had to have perfect confidence that no one was gaining fame or making money from or in the fellowship. A wise decision, it seems to me.

The Twelfth Tradition then goes deeper. It reads: "Anonymity is the spiritual foundation of all our traditions, ever reminding us to place principles before personalities." "The Twelve and Twelve" elaborates: "the spiritual substance of anonymity is sacrifice," the giving up of personal ambition for the common good. It concludes that "anonymity is real humility at work. . . . Moved by the spirit of anonymity, we try to give up our personal desires for prestige as A.A. members both among fellow alcoholics and before the general public." No gurus *in* A.A., and no gurus speaking *for* A.A.

Sacrifice. Humility. Anonymity as a spiritual foundation. These lead me to align anonymity with the unitive way, broadly characterized by growth in selfless love, as we saw earlier. The word "selfless" caught my attention. It may offer us another, more interior way of understanding anonymity.

Never mind not appearing on billboards or on *Oprah.* Never mind not wanting to be known as "Miss A.A." in my group, or as a saint in my community or family (no chance!). How about not acting or "perform-ing" good deeds for the benefit or approval of that ever-present spectator—myself? This kind of selflessness is what Jesus meant when he said, "Do not let your left hand know what your right hand is doing" (Mt. 6:3). Let your deeds be anonymous even to yourself. It is what Buddhists mean when they characterize the enlightened person as having "a beginner's mind," or the "ordinary mind," the mind that does not deem oneself as worthy of particular attention, one's own or anyone else's.

The words of Jesus and the Buddha are meant first of all to counteract the blight of spiritual pride. It is a blight that strikes when, having pruned the more fla-grantly selfish manifestations of our character defects, we mistakenly think that our progress in the spiritual life is something to be proud about, something for which we deserve credit. More deviously, recognizing that this is not the case, it takes self-satisfied pleasure, not humble delight—there is a fine line between the two—in having been "singled out" for "gifts." It asks, Why me? with the secret suspicion that the warrant for the gifts is some-thing "special" about me.

But Jesus' and the Buddha's words are not merely admonitory. They also promise a healthy freedom. I mean, haven't you, in a fit of self-congratulation over some good deed or accomplishment—even one unknown to others—experienced a kind of spiritual/emotional condition something like the sickish feeling of having eaten too many sweets? You know that what you are engaged in is not altogether salutary. Wouldn't you like that ever-present spectator, yourself, to go to sleep, or at least shut up for a while, even when she is saying wonderful things about you? Her self-approving voice can be, in its own register, as troublesome as that of the little critic, the little judge, who scrutinizes our every act for its flaws. No wonder. They both belong to our needy little ego whose horizon is determined by itself and which measures our deeds, others, and the world by their effects on itself. What a small world. What a constricting vision.

So that is the freedom I am thinking of, a freedom from that kind of self-centered, self-conscious thinking. But selflessness as a way of being is a tall order. Purposely working at it, as I read somewhere years ago, is rather like trying to turn lead into gold by following the formula, "You absolutely must not think of a white bear." I make no claim whatsoever to having reached it.

But I have caught glimpses of what it might be like in moments of self-*forgetfulness,* where I have, as it were, unintentionally misplaced my ego, lost it for a little while. An impulse for a generous act comes unbidden. The deed is done easily, spontaneously, graciously, with no thought of oneself but only of the other. Gratitude for the deed, the winning of affection or approval for it, the recognition of it by others seem beside the point. And when the ego reappears on the scene, surprised that this was done without its instigation, supervision, or applause, it has, for once, nothing to say, and might even be slightly amused. It is a curious experience.

This kind of selflessness is, I think, another of the precious freedoms that A.A. members seek when we ask in the Third Step prayer to be relieved "of the bondage of self." It is the freedom of an anonymity in which the right hand doesn't know what the left hand is doing. And is happier for not knowing.

The Unitive Way,
"Having Had a Spiritual
Awakening"

The Twelfth Step

I WAS SURPRISED WHEN, in preparation for writing this section on spiritual awakening, I reread the chapter on the Twelfth Step in "The Big Book." Of course, I have read it before, but over the years its contents had melded in my mind with what I have heard at meetings, with what "The Twelve and Twelve" has to say about it, and with what I myself think. Entitled "Working with Others," the chapter is entirely devoted to how one is to carry the message to other alcoholics. It suggests when to approach an alcoholic, what to say, how much personal aid to offer in the way of money, jobs, housing, how to help the family of the alcoholic, etc. It does not even *mention* a spiritual awakening.

Then I noted that in the step itself—"Having had a spiritual awakening as a result of these steps, we tried to carry this message to other alcoholics and to practice these principles in all our affairs"—the spiritual awakening is, as it were, taken for granted, appearing in a by-the-way subordinate clause as having already been arrived at. And, it stands in a causal relationship with what follows. That is, this step as laid out is not directed to reaching some pinnacle in the spiritual life to be desired in and for itself, or even to describing what the interior life is like "at the top of the mountain." Spiritual awakening is merely assumed, as the state from which one looks outward to other alcoholics and to life, as the condition for living within a broader horizon than that defined by self-interest.

I was delighted. This emphasis by omission confirmed the intuition I was following that the Twelfth Step belongs to the unitive way, to growth in selfless love. *The Encyclopedia of Catholicism* refers to the observation of Evelyn Underhill, well-known Anglican expert on mysticism, that, as it says, "in the greatest Christian mystics, union becomes not an end in itself but leads quite naturally to selfless service of others." No one, absolutely nc one that I know in A.A., ever talks about mystics or mysticism. But Bill W. claims that "the kind of love that has no price tag on it" is at the heart of Alcoholics Anonymous.

I like the phrase "quite naturally." The opposite of grim, jaw-clenching, self-conscious efforts to practice virtue or do good deeds, it suggests ease, grace, flow. It suggests, again, freedom. With every kind of reluctance, backsliding, and niggardliness, and with abiding interference from my ego, growth in freedom is what I have experienced in A.A., almost in spite of myself you might say. Freedom from, freedom to, freedom for.

For me, and for most, first of all, freedom from the compulsion to drink and the obsession with alcohol; for others, still beset with the desire to drink, the freedom to choose not to drink, no small gift. Next, when I was actually at meetings, I experienced patches of freedom from other kinds of obsessive thinking. Then as my spirit came back to life in the steps and as a result of the program as a whole, my relationship with the God of my understanding was rekindled. I wanted to give over to the care of God my will and my life, that is, those very few things that I can directly influence—mostly my actions and my attitudes—and the many, many things that I cannot. When I succeeded in doing this, I found it was a great blessing no longer to have to run the world, even my little world.

Steps Four through Nine freed me from bitter memories, resentment, from the past as something to be regretted. They began to loosen the shackles of my imprisoning character defects and enabled me to forgive myself and others. Using Step Ten, I experienced a kind of liberation in recognizing when I was wrong and promptly admitting it. Now that I could pray again, the life of prayer and meditation that I had assumed as a nun became even more desirable, as in the Eleventh Step I sought "conscious contact" with a God newly understood and loved. And the anonymity that is the spiritual foundation of the program gave me inklings of what it would be like to live unburdened by concern about what others think of me, or what I think of myself.

Now, in Step Twelve, having been freed *from* and freed *to,* I can be *free for* others, that is, to help them freely, not in obedience to a commandment or from a sense of obligation. In "The Twelve and Twelve," where Bill W. enlarges on Step Twelve, he says:

The wonderful energy it releases and the eager action by which it carries our message to the next suffering alcoholic and which finally translates the Twelve Steps into action upon all our affairs is the payoff, the magnificent reality of Alcoholics Anonymous.

Wonderful energy, eager action, freedom. Don't these make the pursuit of the spiritual life compellingly attractive? They do for me.

"Having had a spiritual awakening." Because of misunderstandings of the term after the publication of *Alcoholics Anonymous,* an appendix to the book in later editions clarifies just what this awakening is. For most, it is not "sudden and spectacular upheavals. . . . an immediate and overwhelming God-consciousness followed at once by a vast change in feeling and outlook." Rather, it is usually experienced as transformations in the alcoholic personality that Bill, borrowing from William James, calls of "the educational variety, because they develop slowly over a period of time," as did mine. He goes on, "Quite often friends of the newcomer are aware of the difference long before he is himself."

This is what I hear described at meetings, usually in this sweet way. "My sponsor told me I had a spiritual awakening," they say. "No burning bushes or bolts of lightning, but"—directly quoting Bill W.—"the educational variety." Like the farmer in Jesus' parable, they wake up one day to find that the seed has sprouted and grown, they "know not how. The earth produces of itself, first the stalk, then the head, then the full grain in the head . . . the harvest has come" (Mk. 4:26–29).

Now, they are, as "The Twelve and Twelve" explains, "able to do, feel, and believe that which [they] could not before on [their] own unaided strength and resources alone." Having been 'granted a gift which amounts to a new state of consciousness and being," they find themselves "in possession of a degree of honesty, tolerance, unselfishness, peace of mind, and love" of which they had thought themselves "quite incapable." So now, finally, freedom from the bondage of self means the freedom to be of service.

When "The Big Book" was written, service was often rendered in extraordinary ways. The existence of A.A. was hardly known and meetings were scarce. There were not nearly as many rehabs as there are now. And so, A.A. members went to hospitals looking for likely candidates. They put alcoholics up in their homes for periods of time. They, judiciously, lent them money, got them jobs, spent hours, days, nights with them.

In a different situation now, our ways of giving service are not so dramatic. True we are at times called upon to do Twelfth-Step work in interventions. Some members list their names and telephone numbers with the A.A. Service Boards to be given out to alcoholics calling into them for help. Mostly, we go to meetings, listen and speak at meetings, welcome newcomers, give them our telephone numbers, offer them rides, help with setting up chairs and making coffee, sponsor people, talk to them on the telephone, go through the steps with them, go out speaking, assume positions of responsibility in our groups, or in the regional and national structures of Alcoholics Anonymous. On the one hand, it doesn't seem like much, does it. On the other, every little bit of it contributes to making A.A.'s mission to the suffering alcoholic as effective as it is.

I have been thinking all week of Tina, an old-timer even when I joined our group; she moved last year to a town several hours away. I can see her as I saw her at meeting after meeting—the back of her short-cropped white hair, sitting in her rather squat way right up front next to whatever beginner she had in tow at the time. Last Sunday night a friend of hers told me that Tina still calls Inez, her sponsee who is confined to her home by emphysema, every day. I clarified, "*She* calls Inez?" "Yes," said Mary.

Tina hardly ever spoke without describing herself in the words of "The Big Book" as "happy, joyous and free." With her flat Chicago As, she told us again and again, how happy she was that she no longer had to drink. Of course, she never mentioned the scores of people that she has helped over the years. But when she celebrated her last anniversary with us, I wrote her a card, a custom that some follow at anniversaries. I said, and I meant it, that I would gladly change places with her as she met St. Peter at the Pearly Gates attended by the spirits of all those people. Now I think that Tina doesn't have to wait for her reward. It is surely also because of them that she is happy, joyous, and free.

After the section in "The Twelve and Twelve" dealing with the nature of a spiritual awakening and carrying the message—only five pages in all—"comes the biggest question yet. What about the practice of these principles in *all* our affairs?" asks Bill. How, outside of A.A., do we deal with personal relationships, with our jobs, with "the calamities that befall us in life," with our desires—our instincts—"for emotional security, and wealth, for personal prestige and power, for romance, and for family satisfactions?" In a full twelve pages he then lays out the answers for us situation by situation. Often he calls to witness the simple fact that A.A. members *have* dealt successfully with these matters and shows how the practice of the steps and the program makes this possible. Just as often, he counsels that the answer is—surprise—"still more spiritual development."

He summarizes the fruits of this development in a wonderful paragraph.

Service, gladly rendered, obligations squarely
met, troubles well accepted or solved with
God's help, the knowledge that at home or in
the world we are partners in a common effort,
the well-understood fact that in God's sight all
human beings are important, the proof that
love freely given surely brings a full return, the
certainty that we are no longer alone in self-
constructed prisons, the surety that we need no
longer be square pegs in round holes but can fit
in God's scheme of things—these are the perma-
nent and legitimate satisfactions of right living
for which no amount of pomp and circumstance, no heap of material possessions, could
possibly be substitutes. True ambition is not
what we thought it was. True ambition is the
deep desire to live usefully and walk humbly
under the grace of God.

We have come a long way from the description of the
alcoholic as "childish, emotionally sensitive, and grandiose." The anonymous alcoholic, "a day at a time," and
claiming "spiritual progress, not spiritual perfection" has
found a degree of freedom from the desires for power,
money, and prestige. She has looked for and found emotional stability in her relationship with her Higher

Power. She has not been concerned so much with "personal growth" as with growing up, and thus has discovered not her "inner child" but, as I like to think of it, her inner adult.

I am aware as I write this that A.A. and other Twelve-Step programs have at times been criticized for being too self-centered, for engaging in navel gazing and neglecting matters of social concern like poverty, racism, hunger, and homelessness. It is true that as a fellowship, we have "but one primary purpose—to carry [A.A.'s] message to the alcoholic who still suffers," as the Fifth Tradition says. And I have no idea what other members do personally in these matters.

What I do know is that sober members of Alcoholics Anonymous no longer add to the *deficit* column of the common good. No longer job absentees or unemployed, no longer responsible for harming or killing others in car accidents, no longer engaged in violent acts at home or in public, no longer jailbirds, they save society billions of dollars annually, to put the matter in the crassest terms. And I have no doubt that they are better family members, more productive workers, responsible citizens, and, if they choose, dedicated members of their religious bodies.

Now, one more observation. I must mention again Bill W.'s insight in that hotel in Akron. In his desperation, he somehow knew that working with others was the solution to his drinking problem. He did not know at first—as we who follow after him do not know but come to learn—that helping others to sobriety is also a source of pure joy. The reciprocity buried deep within human nature itself begins in need and flowers into gladness at the well-being of others.

"What goes around comes around," as the saying goes. Or, as the Christian scriptures put it, "you reap whatever you sow" (Gal. 6:7). "Give and it will be given to you. A good measure, pressed down, shaken together, running over will be put into your lap" (Lk. 6:38).

The Twelve Traditions

A Mustard Seed

> With what can we compare the kingdom of God, or
> what parable will we use for it? It is like a mustard seed
> which, when sown upon the ground, is the smallest of all
> seeds upon earth. yet when it is sown it grows up and
> becomes the greatest of all shrubs, and puts forth large
> branches, so that the birds of the air can make nests in its
> shade.   (MK. 4:30–32)

B ILL W. AND DR. BOE
first met in 1935. By the time of the publication of *Alcoholics Anonymous* four years later, there were about one
hundred men and women in A.A. At the end of 1941,
there were eight thousand members. Today, according to
the statistics on the AA.org web site, there are estimated
to be 1,989,124 A.A. members in 98,710 groups around
the world. How did this little seed grow? How, in
heaven's name, did "an erratic band of alcoholics" man-
age to work together and nurture it in a world where, as

Bill W. says, "the struggle for wealth, power, and prestige was tearing humanity apart" just as it is now? They had the steps to guide them in their personal lives. What practices and principles did they adopt for the fellowship? The answers to these questions are found in the Twelve Traditions. They lay out the guiding principles of every A.A. group and of Alcoholics Anonymous as a whole.

My group celebrated its fifty-fourth anniversary in 1999. Two window-shadelike lists, one bearing the steps, the other the traditions, are displayed at the front of one of the rooms where we meet. They look old enough to have been there from the beginning. For years I hardly noticed them. Unlike some groups, mine does not hold meetings devoted to the traditions. So it did not occur to me to wonder how my group or A.A. as a whole worked. The meetings were there. So were the coffee, the leaders and speakers, and the literature. I received notices of the monthly anniversaries and incoming and outgoing speaking commitments in the mail. Someone gave me a booklet put out by something called Intergroup, listing times and places of meetings, over fifteen hundred in the greater metropolitan area where I live. I heard the Preamble (a kind of condensation of the traditions, I realized later) read at the beginning of meetings: "Alcoholics Anonymous is a fellowship of men and women who share their experience, strength and hope with each other. . . ."

Then my sponsor was named group chair—no glass ceilings here. I became vaguely aware that all the positions in the group are held on a rotating basis. They change at a business meeting held every six months, the term of office "The Twelve and Twelve" recommends as a safeguard against entrenched power.

Accustomed to the long silences when volunteers are solicited for tasks at non-A.A. meetings I attend, I was surprised that when it came time in my women's group for someone new to take over the coffee-making, an old-timer quickly came forward because, she told us, it was the month of her anniversary. She wanted to express her gratitude in a concrete way.

And, when I was slow to follow this kind of example, happy, joyous, and free Tina "volunteered" me to be the person responsible for getting guest speakers for open meetings. She took me to the peculiar gathering of my A.A. counterparts from other groups in the area. Every three months, on a Saturday morning at a school in a nearby town, these group representatives mill around in a loosey-goosey manner, trading commitments—we'll send you a speaker for a step meeting, we need two for an open meeting—and then get people from their groups to fill them.

Of course there are problems, personality conflicts, disagreements about how things are to be done. How could there not be? About fifteen years ago a serious dispute arose in my group over whether we should direct some of our surplus funds to the support of a halfway house on whose board some of our members, devoted A.A.s, served. It was such a good cause, they said. The residents came to our meetings. We would only be helping them get sober.

The suggestion seemed to others to be in direct violation of the Sixth Tradition: "An A.A. group ought never endorse, finance, or lend the A.A. name to any related facility or outside enterprise, lest problems of money, property, and prestige divert us from our primary purpose." The board members didn't think any of those things applied in this case. The only obstacle seemed to be the tradition itself, an abstraction standing in the way of the very concrete good that they, with the best will in the world, wanted to achieve. To me it seemed that the proposal was already shattering group unity and causing the very kind of problem the tradition was designed to avoid. And what would happen when other members proposed the next worthy cause for our consideration, in competition, perhaps, for our limited funds?

The group conscience meetings became rancorous. An anonymous letter, maligning several board members, was distributed. The General Service Office in New York City was called. The call was referred to one of the eleven (out of eighty-five) staff members who belong to A.A., and whose jobs are to deal with matters like these. These eleven also hold their positions on a rotating basis. They will never dictate a course of action, but the opinion given was that the proposal was contrary to the Sixth Tradition. The suggestion was withdrawn.

The other night after a meeting I overheard two of the board members talking about a fund-raising campaign for the halfway house and a "sober house" that has been founded since. The project has not only survived but flourished. However painful the memories of the episode are for all who were involved, I think we did the right thing.

Out of disagreements less serious than this—desires or needs not being met, for instance, and the group unwilling to change—new groups sprout up and grow. Bill W. said that this kind of "heresy" is a good thing as long as it results in more meetings. Some A.A.s individually leave one group to join another. They are free to do that. Sometimes new meetings branch out amicably enough under the auspices of the parent group. In the mid-eighties, my sponsor brought me to a meeting that she and a few other women were beginning out of a desire for a meeting during the day, not at night. At first there were only five or six of us present. Today, every Monday, Wednesday, and Friday at noon, you can find twenty-five to thirty A.A.s, men and women—some from our group, some not, it doesn't matter—in the chapter room of another church in town for a "Big Book" or step meeting.

You can read the list of the Twelve Traditions at the beginning of this book or a fuller account of them in "The Twelve and Twelve." Please do. Here is a rough summary of them. No requirements for membership "except a desire. . . ." No rules and regulations for members. No dues or fees. No fund-raising. No acceptance of large gifts. No established hierarchies. No one with the authority to tell anyone or any group what to do or think or believe. No one with the power to kick you out. No professional, paid A.A.s. No establishment of facilities for the treatment of alcoholism. No mergers with, endorsement of, or lobbying of other groups or causes, even, or especially those concerned with the disease of alcoholism—medical, educational, religious, political, legislative. No PR or membership drives.

And here, broadly, is what the traditions recommend. "Our common welfare" above all. "The least possible leadership," under "only one authority, a loving God as He may express Himself in our group conscience." A membership open to all who want it. Only one primary purpose. Personal and group autonomy (freedom). "Corporate poverty," by which is meant "that A.A. must always stay poor," with only the financial resources for "bare running expenses plus a prudent reserve." Nonprofessionalism. Public relations guided by "the principle of attraction rather than promotion." And personal anonymity in our relations with the general public. I mean, were those early A.A.s crazy? Is this any way to run an organization?

They, full of the zeal of the newly converted, didn't think so at first. They were also full of bright ideas about how to carry A.A.'s message. And like everybody else— Bill says even more so—they were susceptible to the lure of wealth and power and prestige. So, some "elder states-men" tried holding on to positions of responsibility in their groups, since they, of course, knew better than any-one else how things should work. Others were tempted to become professional, paid, Twelfth-Steppers, putting their A.A. experience to good use while at the same time solv-ing their own financial problems. For a while, in the very early days, fearful for A.A.'s reputation, they catered only to "pure alcoholics." "So, beggars, tramps, asylum inmates, prisoners, queers, plain crackpots, and fallen women were definitely out." They almost expelled a vociferous atheist who, "distressingly enough ... proceeded to stay sober."

even though he couldn't "stand this God stuff!" Strapped for cash, they deliberated long and hard over whether to take a $10,000 bequest. One group built a big, multi-purpose A.A. center. Some became "A.A. show-offs" on the radio and TV. You get the picture.

In every case, these ventures either failed or were rejected as options in what came to be known as group conscience meetings. The bright ideas threatened the freedom of individuals or groups, undermined trust, especially where money and prestige were involved, and/or eroded the unity of the fellowship in its mission to every suffering alcoholic. "The Twelve and Twelve," in story after story (like "The Big Book," "The Twelve and Twelve" carries its points home by stories) tells us how the traditions "were hammered out on the anvils of experience[s]" like these.

Thomas E. Clarke, S.J., in an article I read some-where years ago, refers to the traditions as "graced struc-tures." They are that in themselves, eschewing as they do the pomp and circumstance of the world, the worldly view of how things work and succeed. What amazes me is that the early A.A.s somehow had the wisdom to adopt them and to avoid the shoals on which the most worthy causes, espoused by well-intentioned people, have foundered—dissension, the lure of power, money, fame, even when sought after for the apparent good of the whole. The claim to have the truth, the whole truth, and nothing but the truth.

As best I can figure out now, the founders of A.A. came to understand and act out of four basic desires or insights. The first, the most fundamental, foundational, desire was this: No matter what their worries about the future or the reputation of A.A., or their beliefs or opinions on anything, A.A. members desired sobriety for everyone. *They could not bring themselves to doom any alcoholic to the terrible suffering of and possible death from the disease of alcoholism.* Even that cantankerous atheist had to be left free to believe as he wished if he could be helped to stay sober. Unity in pursuit of this mission was seen as crucial, the real bottom line, more necessary by far than financial resources which, hand in hand with power, so often tend to divide rather than unite.

They knew that they were entrusted with "a spiritual entity"—Bill calls it that—with nurturing "a seed" in the "kingdom of God," *not* with building an organization. They were stewards, farmers, not empire builders. The seed would grow under the influence of the Spirit of God in the conscience of the individual and in our group conscience. And, not least important, they knew themselves to be deeply flawed individuals who needed protection from their own worst selves. They were, in other words, humble.

But that is only half the story. History, including the history of religious communities and institutions, is replete with stories of the loss or betrayal of the vision of the founders, sometimes even before their death. How has A.A. succeeded where others have failed, putting forth "large branches" for every possible kind of bird's nest, and every kind, color, and plumage of bird? As individuals and as a fellowship we try to conduct ourselves in accord with the steps and the traditions not because they are dictated to us by people in authority but because we know that our lives and the life of our groups depend on obedience to them. "Great suffering and great love are A.A.'s disciplinarians; we need no others," says Bill.

According to Webster's dictionary, a tradition is "the handing down of information, beliefs, and customs by word of mouth or by example from one generation to another without written instruction." It is the right word for how I learned the A.A. way of doing things. And it is just the right word for the way A.A. grew, grows. And it is because of the traditions that this book carries the pen name "Sister Molly Monahan" on its title page.

Second Spring

Sin and Salvation

O<small>VER</small> <small>TWENTY</small> <small>YEARS</small> <small>AGO,</small>
when I was living at a retreat center that my community
sponsored in the foothills of the Catskills, a plague of
locusts came through the land. They advanced in multi-
tudes through the countryside—you could hear them
chewing their way—denuding every tree, bush, and
shrub in sight. The lush green foliage clothing the hills in
my view gave way to bare, brown branches, nary a leaf
in sight.

Then to my surprise, several weeks after the plague
passed, the hills gradually began to show again a covering

of light olive green. I do not know how it happens. I had not thought it possible. A second growth. A second spring.

Just so, after the ravages brought on me by my alcoholism, my spirit came to life again in Alcoholics Anonymous, slowly, tentatively, questioning. My questions were not about the truth of my basic Catholic beliefs—in sin, salvation, in Jesus as my savior; I had always believed them to be true. Of course, I had committed sins, and believed, in some theoretical fashion (what Newman calls notional rather than real assent, as I said earlier), that the death of Jesus had won forgiveness and salvation for me. But I don't know that I ever *felt* myself lost and in need of being saved in any deep way.

That's *just* how I felt in the throes of my alcoholism. And the experience of being saved in A.A., and of being grateful to God for it, was, and is, undeniably real. It was this experienced reality that made me wonder *how real* my belief in these Christian truths was. How truly did I know myself a sinner? What is sin? How do I *experience* salvation? Am I really grateful for my salvation from sin, as grateful as I am for my recovery in A.A.? How do I know Jesus, who is never mentioned in A.A., as my savior?

The other day I asked my older sister whether she still remembered the Act of Contrition that we learned as children. We said it after telling our sins to the priest in confession every Saturday. Yes, she said firmly, she did. And at breakneck speed, in one breath as it were, she said: "OmyGod amheartilysorryforhavingoffendedThee, andIdetestallmys nsbecauseIdreadthelossofheavenandthe painsofhell,butm ostofallbecausetheyoffendThee,myGod, whoartallgoodar ddeservingofallmylove.Ifirmlyresolve withthehelpof Thygracetoconfessmysins,todopenance,and toamendmylife. Amen."

I laughed to myself. She was saying the prayer in just the way that I play a piano piece resurrected from my childhood repertoire: If I stop for one moment to think what I am doing, I am lost. I did not ask my sister whether she still says the Act of Contrition, or when she last went to confession, where the prayer is less frequently used. But I know that I have not said it in years. And like many Catholics, even other nuns, I go to confession now only two or three times a year, usually before a big feast like Christmas or Easter.

What has happened to weekly confession, to the daily examination of conscience, or the "examen," practiced by me twice daily as a young nun? These observances, along with others, have all but disappeared from Catholic life (and vowed religious life) since Vatican II— some with good reason, some not. But then, one may ask, what has happened to sin? And if the sense of sin, of sinfulness, has been diminished, what has happened to redemption, to the joy and gratitude that come from knowing oneself saved?

Of course, I thought that as a cradle Catholic I knew what sin was. And I vividly remember my first experience of it. It was Christmas morning, not long after my first communion, and the very strict rules of fasting before communion, still in effect then, had been drilled into us by the good nuns. I had gotten a play doctor's set as a present, containing a stethoscope, tongue depressors, cotton balls, and little bottles of candy pills. Without thinking, on Christmas morning before mass, I popped one of the pills into my mouth. I had broken my fast and could not receive holy communion. But how could I *not* go to communion on Christmas day? Already ashamed of my offense, it never occurred to me to ask my parents or one of the nuns about my dilemma. What was I to do?

I worried about my plight all during mass and by the time communion came I had my solution. I left my pew, feigning sickness, and went to the vestibule at the back of the church. But Mrs. Shea, the mother of one of my classmates, no doubt thinking it a pity that I should miss communion on Christmas day, followed me, took me by the hand, and led me back into the church and up to the communion rail. Miserable, I followed her and received the host. Double indemnity. I do not remember for how long I lived with the guilty knowledge of my "sin," or if I told my parents exactly what was troubling me. My next memory is of the young parish priest, a friend of the family, sitting on the edge of my bed one night, and hearing my tearful confession.

Take this little tale as a paradigm of all the rules and regulations of the Catholic Church in those days before Vatican II: about attendance at Sunday mass; not eating meat on Friday; about the partial fast observed during Lent and prescribed in allowed ounces; making your Easter duty, etc.—all obligations omitted "under pain of sin." Add the commandments of God, especially in the legalistic manner we were taught about them, and especially about matters sexual, apply them in slide-rule fashion to normal childhood, adolescent, and young adult development, and to adulthood itself, and you have plenty of occasions of sin, plenty of cause for guilt of a certain kind, and plenty of need for confession. So it was then. So it is not now.

And so it was, in spades, in the life of nuns before Vatican II. In addition to the obligations assumed in making vows of chastity, poverty, and obedience, also approached legalistically in a "catechism of the vows," there were rules and regulations galore. I remember thinking, under an especially strict superior who regularly posted prescribing notices on the bulletin board about every facet of our young lives, that from the moment I put my foot on the floor in the morning until I got into bed at night, there was a right and a wrong way for me to do *everything*. I myself during one period got a daily correction from her, like a vitamin, one a day. And I was bound by my egoistic desire for perfection, held up to us as an ideal, to get it all right. Of course I didn't.

That is all gone, too, and most of it with good reason. We were—I was—seriously misconstruing things. To make a rather black-and-white case of it, we were, for all our talk about the grace of God, practically ignoring Jesus' and the apostle Paul's injunctions against seeking salvation in the law and its many prescriptions, thinking to win salvation by our own efforts. We were as well confusing rules and regulations with practices: The first, as I said before, to be kept because some authority dictates them; the second, as meaningful acts of devotion or discipline. So, for instance, I do fast now before reception of the eucharist but as an act of preparatory reverence, not because of a church law which it is a sin to break.

On the other hand, all of this "sinning" was played out against the backdrop of our having been saved in some basic way by the death and resurrection of Jesus Christ, salvation made available to us by baptism into the Roman Catholic Church. I was given the impression that everybody else, even other Christians, were lost and would never enter the gates of heaven opened for us by Christ, our savior. We alone had been washed clean of the stain of original sin; we were adopted children of God, members of the Mystical Body of Christ. By virtue of our baptism, and as long as we did not commit a mortal sin, we were in the state of grace; the Holy Trinity dwelt within our souls. Our duty was to be believing, practicing Catholics, to give good example to others, and so one day to go to heaven, where our reward awaited us. Except for the exclusivity of our claims and some of the imagery—the stain on our soul, the gates of heaven opening and closing—I do not deny the truth and beauty of these beliefs today. (Unfortunately, in my opinion, Catholics do not hear much anymore about the Mystical Body and the indwelling of the Trinity, the latter a notion of the God within held in some form by many of the great world religions.)

The problem with my understanding here, however, besides the triumphalism that it engendered, was that it had a certain mechanistic quality to it. With baptism we Catholics were automatically saved, as it were, and sins were wrong acts that we committed from time to time. Giving good example, which I heard regularly preached by a young priest not too long ago, has always seemed to me a kind of self-satisfied posturing, like the Pharisee in Jesus' parable recounting his good deeds before God and others in the temple (Lk. 18:10–13). But where in all of this, as we lived out our lives after baptism, was the *experience* of our woundedness acknowledged and our deep, deep need for God and God's grace conveyed to us? And if we had such experiences, as all human beings do, how were they connected for us to sin, to grace, to salvation?

As it is now, most of those rules and regulations no longer hold in religious life or in the Catholic Church, and like members of the mainline churches in general we do not hear much about sin and sinfulness—certainly no more fire and brimstone sermons about "a sinner in the hands of an angry God."

It is true that there have been theological advances made in our understanding of sin since Vatican II, especially, I would note, of what is called social sin. Social sin names the injustices that inhere in the very structures of society itself—global society now—begetting poverty, prejudice, inequality, and in which white middle-class educated Americans like me are indeed complicit. In some parishes, one does hear sermons about this. And in the documents of Vatican II and long, painstaking interreligious conversations since, the Catholic teaching on the place of other religious traditions in God's plan for the salvation of all people has been modified so that heaven is no longer a Catholic ghetto! But if I judge by my own experience, we do not get much help from church in understanding and realizing either our personal sin or our salvation.

In our day also, popular psychology tries to explain, or explain away, a lot of what we used to think of as sin, finding its causes in our upbringing, and crediting our guilt to the tyranny of an overdeveloped superego, a true enough assessment in some cases. Genetic research puts the blame for wrong action on our genes. Our culture, permissive and self-indulgent in the extreme, has lost almost all notion of sin, so that now, but for different reasons, we are again, or still, desensitized to our sinfulness and our need for God's grace.

I would guess that Anthony Bloom, commenting on the Gospel verse, "knock and the door will be opened for you" (Mt. 7:7), captures the state of mind of many churchgoers: "Before you knock at the door, you must realize that you are outside. If you spend your time imagining that you are already in the kingdom of God, there is certainly no point in knocking at any door for it to be opened. . . ." We're not really sinners, we think. We are just nice people who slip up now and then.

But on this count, I think that Luther got it right, or at least put it in a way that is helpful to me. We are always, not just when we *commit* a sin, *simul justus et pecca-tor*—at the very same time both sinners and just, working out our salvation in fear and trembling, "a day at a time," as we A.A.s say of our sobriety. I know this now not as some theoretical doctrine but in a real, lived way. And I learned it, am still learning it, through my alcoholism and in the fellowship of Alcoholics Anonymous.

No, I should say more truthfully, I realize this and other things about my alcoholism better than I do about my sinfulness. I know from the sad stories I have heard from or about others who have had relapses, even after years of sobriety, that I am *always* in recovery, never cured; that if I denied my alcoholism and began drinking, I would lose all the good things in my life. I know that alcoholism is a fatal disease, a matter of life and death. People die long, slow deaths from it, or kill themselves by overdosing, or kill themselves and/or others in accidents that happen when they are under the influence. It is not uncommon to hear A.A. members tell of having attempted suicide, and I have known alcoholics/addicts (almost everyone under a certain age in A.A. today has experimented with or used drugs) who have died this tragic death. Short of physical death, active alcoholism means death to the spirit, to peace of mind, freedom, to right relations with others, not to mention the loss of jobs, family, and self-respect.

And finally, I know that I cannot stay sober alone, cannot save myself. It is in reliance on God's power, most commonly as it is mediated to me through others in A.A., that I am saved, safe. But, in that always peculiar mix that we call the mystery of free will and grace, I also know that my "salvation" depends on my own choices, especially in being faithful to my A.A. program.

By analogy then with my disease, this is what I think sinfulness looks like, what we all look like in our sinful state; these are the lineaments of the visage we bear as children of Adam and Eve, the marks of what we call original sin. 1) Our sinfulness is always destructive, death-dealing in some way to ourselves and others, and salvation, conversely, is a matter of the fullness of life, and now, not just in the hereafter. 2) We cannot save ourselves by ourselves. We are utterly dependent on the love, and power, and goodness of a God who is willing to help us, and we need others to bring us to this knowledge and to this loving power. 3) And, not least important, perhaps, we rarely know, or realize, all of the above.

At any rate, that is how it is with me. I am often in denial. I do not see what is really the case. For all the talk we hear about God's love for us these days, much more than when I was growing up, I do not always clearly see that God cares for me, desires good for me—loves me. Perhaps Jesus is the only one who ever really believed it from his birth, one way to understand why he is called and is, in Catholic belief, the Son of God.

And like alcoholics, including me, who only realized how sick we were when we began to get better, maybe that is why the saints seem to become more conscious of their sinfulness as they grow in the love of God and in their conviction of God's love for them. Because it is only in the apprehension of that love that sin is revealed for what it is, a refusal, or a denial, of love. Perhaps this is what was meant by the saying I once heard, that we need to have our sinfulness *revealed* to us, just as we do the other truths of our faith.

In such an accounting of sin, God is not an impersonal lawgiver, or a policeman waiting to catch us out in a bad deed, or even someone somehow "offended" by our transgressions, as the Act of Contrition put it. God is, rather, like the father in the parable of the Prodigal Son (Lk. 15:11–32): grieved to see us harming ourselves and others; waiting for us to come to our senses; and rejoicing to see us (re)turn to him.

Salvation, then, understood as an ever-growing living into that love, now and in its fullness in the hereafter, *is* reason for gratitude and joy. And, as Bill Wilson knew—as I, too, have experienced in A.A.—I am grateful, happy, and at peace in those moments when I am enabled to love and act lovingly toward others—that deep reciprocity again. This is what true happiness is. But too often we imagine that our salvation, our happiness, lies elsewhere—in the phantoms of power, money, sex, prestige. Or in the love of other persons from whom we ask too much, since they are, alas, as limited and as flawed (and as mortal) as we ourselves are.

It used to annoy me to hear some of the men in our group say, repeatedly, "I thought I was just a nice guy who drank too much." They meant that they had not yet faced up to their character defects and all the harm they had done to themselves and to others. After a long while, I realized that that was just what I thought about *myself*. I was just a nice nun who drank too much. Not so. And just as I gradually learned that alcoholism means more than drinking too much, so it is also clear to me, especially clear as I am writing this, that I am, in fact, a sinner.

I have never committed murder, or adultery, or theft. But I can be in the course of any given day resentful, critical, stingy, lazy, contemptuous, jealous, angry, unforgiving, uncaring. I am guilty of one or some of these dispositions, usually not all at once, though they do by their nature tend to come in clusters, one begetting the other. This sinful self of mine is not a happy self. These are not happy words. They do not describe happy frames of mind. They are corrosive, destructive, not only of those toward whom they are directed but of me and of my peace and well-being.

It is my hard heart, my "heart of stone" as Ezekiel called it, that is driving me at these times. I need God and God's grace to give me a new heart, "a heart of flesh" (Ez. 36:26). And if I, as a Christian, am to know myself loved by God as Jesus knew himself to be, and if I am to love others as Jesus enjoined, "Just as I have loved you, you also should love one another" (Jn. 13:34)—I need to find the heart of Jesus in myself.

The Easter Vigil liturgy, in a reference to the sin of Adam and Eve, says, O felix culpa . . . "O happy fault which gained for us such and so great a redeemer." My alcoholism has been for me a felix culpa. Sin-ridden as it was, it has brought me to a new knowledge and love of Jesus, my redeemer.

The Lamb of God

I<small>N</small> JANUARY 1993, THE
month in which I marked my tenth anniversary in A.A.
and the thirty-seventh anniversary of my profession of
vows, I was at Sunday mass in the Basilica of St. Agnes
outside of Rome. It is a beautiful little seventh-century
church, built supposedly on the site of the grave of St.
Agnes (the name means "lamb") outside of the Porta Pia
on the outskirts of the city. We were celebrating the feast
of the Baptism of Jesus and in the Gospel reading for the
day John the Baptist hails Jesus as "the Lamb of God

who takes away the sins of the world." The sermon was, of course, in Italian, which I could more or less follow.

Whatever the fervent young priest really said, in my journal I recorded that "I understood him to be talking about Jesus [the Lamb] bearing the *peso* [the weight] of our sin. I understood that it is the Christ within me who is absorbing and taking the sting out of my sin. And further, multivalently, that I am 'lamb'. . . . And along with this, for which I am most grateful, a 'revelation' of myself as childish, possessive, jealous, etc. . . . It is humiliating, or humbling."

I had long been familiar with the biblical account of the sacrifice of the paschal lamb whose blood saved the Israelites from slavery and death on the first Passover. That passage in Exodus 12 informed one of the earliest Christian theologies of the death of Jesus as salvific, and of the eucharist as a reenactment of that death in a sacrificial meal. The image of the Lamb of God occurs four times in every mass, five times when the Gloria is recited or sung. How many thousands of times had I heard it in my lifetime? For some reason, it all came home to me in my experience in the Basilica of St. Agnes on that Sunday outside of Rome, listening to a sermon in a language that I could barely understand.

There was nothing spectacular or spooky about the experience. Perhaps you have been similarly touched by a sermon or some other event. No doubt, the coincidence of the name and site of the church and the particular Gospel reading for the day contributed to its impact on me. For whatever reason, the experience stayed with me. I can't quite explain it, but for months afterwards when I was feeling sad, or burdened, or hurt, or unhappy with myself, I needed only to reach inside to Jesus the Lamb of God within me, as me, to find comfort and forgiveness. Maybe it was the case that I was able to forgive myself.

"A grace given is given once and for all," says my spiritual director. A year and a few months later, my journal records: "You take away (if I ask you let you) my constant fault-finding. You take away my hard, little, bitter, crab-apple heart and give me a big, warm, juicy watermelon heart." I had begun to understand that the "taking away" does not happen by some spiritual trade-off where Jesus "pays for" my sins or appeases an angry Father God. Or opens the gates of heaven. Or washes the "stain" of original sin off my soul in the water of baptism. Salvation doesn't happen automatically. It happens because I want to and am enabled to change by faith in the Christ within me, as that faith is enacted in my life.

Strange as it seems, I did not immediately express any of this to myself in terms of salvation as I have just explained it. Again, it was my A.A. experience of having been saved by a loving God, with no reference whatsoever to Jesus, that led me to wonder how he fit into the picture, how I as a Christian knew *him* as my savior. I had the answer as it were before I had the question. It was some time before I saw that Jesus as the Lamb of God offered me a way of understanding my salvation as something real in my life now. Salvation was no longer abstract for me, a dogma to which I gave intellectual assent and which I would experience at last in heaven. I was able to match the language of my beliefs with my own lived, felt experience.

And then I understood my baptism anew as well. (Would you believe it was only a moment ago that I realized that the seed of this insight was planted on the feast of the Baptism of Jesus?) At my baptism I was made a child of God, called to be a follower of Jesus, the Son of God. This is my vocation as a Christian, as others are called by God in other ways. But just as I have learned in A.A. that I need others to help me stay sober and to believe and trust in God, I need the members of my church to witness to their faith in Christ, the "way, the truth, and the life" (Jn. 14:6) for me, and to help me live my life as a Christian. As the post–Vatican II ritual for the sacrament makes clear, I am baptized *into* a community, which community promises at the time to nurture and support me in that faith. I in turn then bear the same responsibility toward others.

As it is, my experience of Jesus in the image of the Lamb of God within me is at least once removed, in the way that images are, from the realization of a man dying a terrible death on a cross for my sake. I have not yet come to terms with that love as real in my life. "No one has greater love than this, to lay down one's life for one's friends" (Jn. 15:13), a death that also reveals that "God so loved the world that he gave his only son" for us (Jn. 3:16). Such a great love may be too much for me, more reality than I can yet bear. It may seem to ask too much from me, to be too costly. What kind of a person would I have to be to love others like that, to love them as Christ has loved me, as God loves me?

But we have in the Gospels not only an account of Jesus' passion, death, and resurrection. We have his life, very specific accounts of a very specific personality. I have a friend, a deeply religious man, Catholic in bone and marrow. I had known that like the woman in A.A. who prays only to Mary he finds the life of his spirit in her. I admit I was a bit shocked when he told me once in a telephone conversation that he doesn't like Jesus. We did not discuss the matter then and have not since. Does he read Jesus the way Pasolini does in his film on Matthew's Gospel, ranting and raving all over the place?

I don't like that Jesus either. But whatever one thinks of his sentiment, Jesus is real to my friend; he is not a cardboard Jesus.

My friend's blunt statement made me question what kind of person this Jesus whom I claim to love is. Meditating on the Gospel readings for Lent of last year, I discovered, or discovered anew, a Jesus I admire more and more. Someone who lived in the sheer light of truth and unequivocatingly spoke it. Who was courageous and cared little for what people in authority thought of him. Who, regardless of rules and regulations (about not healing on the Sabbath, for instance), saw with compassionate eyes only the real need of the person standing before him, and who welcomed everybody—sinners and the despised in society—into his company (like A.A. in these last two, or rather, we like him). Who exhausted himself in the service of others. Whose touch healed as his word forgave sins.

It is clear to me that in his life as well as in his death, this Jesus claimed to be showing us, revealing to us, the love, the face of his Father. "Whoever has seen me has seen the Father" (Jn. 14:9). And he challenged us, as in the parable of the Good Samaritan, to "go and do likewise"(Lk. 10:37), to love others as he did, as God does. Even without dying for others, living for them in this way seems a tall enough order for me.

Theologian Bernard Lonergan describes our experience of the mystery of the love of God as "a vector, an undertow, a fateful call to a dreaded holiness," dreaded, that is, when we begin to sense what it will ask of us. It feels that way to me as I write this—awful. And about as far as you can get from any ideal of sanctity that I entertained for myself as a young nun. I imagined holiness then as enjoying the sweet bliss of union with God in prayerful solitude. I had no notion of the real cost of the stripping away of self required in a life of deep prayer, not to mention the stripping away of selfishness in a life of service.

Now, a somewhat wiser woman, I don't even think about holiness for myself. I just muddle along, following, however, this intimation. It is, all of it, all the love, of a piece, all one love—of God, of Jesus, of others, of myself. It is all God's love "poured into our hearts through the Spirit" (Rom. 5:5). "God is love. . . . We love because he first loved us" (1 Jn. 4:16,19). Jesus knew this fully; Bill Wilson knew it "in a glass darkly." We need only surrender to it and let it flow through us to others. Only. "A fated call to a dreaded holiness"—wherein, confounding us, lie radical peace and joy.

Religion and Spirituality

"My Name Is Molly and I'm a Catholic"

So, THERE THEY ARE, MY reflections on the spirituality of Alcoholics Anonymous, and the answers that I have to the questions it has raised for me about my Catholic faith. I said in the beginning of this book that without A.A. "not only would I not be in recovery, I would be spiritually bereft." You will understand better now, I trust, that even if I had managed merely to stop drinking, were "dry," and had not dealt with the mental and spiritual aspects of the disease, I would still be miserable.

But I meant more than that. I meant that A.A. has brought new life to me precisely as a Catholic. Unlike those who say "I found spirituality in A.A., not religion," thus separating and opposing the two (I understand what they mean by this, and will deal with it later), I feel blessed to have both in my life. I cannot separate them. My Catholicism is as much a part of my identity as is my alcoholism. It is the mother tongue of my soul, and the "language" of its creed, code, and cult (worship) articulate and give me ways to express the spirituality I find in A.A.

Further, it's not as if the relationship between these two has been or is one-sided. As must be obvious by now, from the beginning I "saw" A.A. spirituality through the lens of my Catholic faith, as it were, and tested it for its soundness against my understanding and appreciation of the Catholic tradition, whether I realized I was doing that or not. So that, while I acknowledge with the deepest gratitude the ways in which A.A. has helped me to grow spiritually, I must also acknowledge that the seeds of its spirituality fell on the rich soil of the ancient Christian tradition in which I was raised. It is no doubt for these reasons that A.A. spirituality alone would never be enough for me, austere as it necessarily is, without signs or symbols or sacraments, without ritual or communal worship, and without expression in the beauty of the art that attends those rituals and adorns places of worship.

As a Catholic, because of my belief in the incarnation of Jesus Christ, his taking on and sanctifying human flesh and all matter, I know that my body, ever so really part of me, is holy too. And it needs to have a part in my worship of God in word, song, gesture. My senses—of seeing, hearing, tasting, touching, smelling—need the spiritual nourishment provided by the music, the sacred vestments and vessels, the bread, wine, water, oils, candles, incense, flowers. They need the painting, frescoes, mosaics, the sculpture inspired by scripture and tradition.

And because I am not only a private person but a social being, I need to worship with others the God who is not only the God of *my* understanding, but *our* God. As a Catholic, I do this primarily in the celebration of the eucharist. There my sisters and brothers and I, as members of the body of Christ incarnate now, are nourished by and give thanks to God through the offering and reception of the bread and wine, which, according to the words of the mass, "become for us the body and blood of Christ."

And for the same kinds of reasons I need the beliefs of my Catholic faith, as Jews may need the Torah and Muslims the Ku'ran. Except for a few places in A.A. literature where God is named or addressed as our Creator, the belief in a Higher Power who loves and cares for us is unelaborated, again, necessarily so, given A.A.'s mission. The mysteries of the Catholic faith—the mystery of the Trinity, of the incarnation of Jesus Christ, of redemption, of resurrection, for example—do not contradict this belief. For me, they strengthen it and give it fuller expression. These beliefs, these hopes—I cannot always separate faith from hope; I believe in order to hope, I hope to believe—are not abstract formulas to which I give mere intellectual assent. In their appeal to my experience, my imagination, my emotions, they are integral to my spirituality, to my prayer—to my life. I mean, rather, that with the help of God's grace I am called to make them so, to *incarnate* them in *my* life.

At the same time, however, I understand and sympathize with the people who say that they have "found spirituality in A.A., not religion." I think by spirituality they mean that they have found a personal relationship with a loving God and a faith that works in their lives. And by religion I think they mean a creed, code, and cult that are largely meaningless to them. Or more negatively, that their failure to live in accord with these three constituents of religion—which they think they have got to do on their own—fills them with guilt and with fear of a punishing God.

I am not going to rehearse in any detail all of the reasons why people, and not only in A.A., find religious institutions spiritually wanting, or worse, off-putting. To paint with a very broad brush, here are some of them: poor preaching; perfunctory worship services; unsympathetic clergy; little by way of adult religious education, especially in the scriptures; little help in the nurture of personal piety and devotion; a wan community life; rigid hierarchical structures; laws and rules and regulations imposed with the injunction that they be obeyed, but without conveying an understanding of their meaning as practices or their purpose as avenues that might lead to peace and freedom; dogmas presented chiefly as the criteria for orthodox belief, and not as mysteries that relate to and illumine our lives.

It is as if "the tree of life" (Rev. 22:2), taken as a symbol of the spirituality to be found in the biblical religious traditions, is surrounded by dead brush or prickly hedgerows. So those who are spiritual seekers go looking to other spiritualities, good and bad, from Heaven's Gate to New Age to the practice of Zen. And others see little in the way that religion presents itself that would awaken a desire for a personal spiritual life in them.

Certainly not because they thought they were looking for it, most people in A.A. find a viable, even vibrant, spirituality. A.A. has found ways of making spirituality attractive and available to all who want it. Its traditions prevent the growth of "hedgerows." Its steps don't threaten punishment but promise serenity. Its simple belief in a Higher Power has room for all, at the same time that it encourages its members to the practice of religion. Its meetings, sponsors, its fellowship encourage and support spiritual growth.

I daydream at times about how some of these features of the fellowship might be adopted and adapted by religious institutions. Parishes, congregations, even religious communities like mine might form "faith support groups" where people "with the desire" to believe or to grow in faith —"Lord, I believe, help my unbelief" (Mk. 9:24)—might share their doubts and fears, and, as the A.A. Preamble says, their "experience, strength, and hope." Perhaps as spiritual companions, like sponsors, people could guide one another through the steps. They might read spiritual books together out loud, as A.A.s read "The Big Book" and "The Twelve and Twelve," and then, as we do, talk not about the ideas in the books but about how the reading does or does not reflect their experience. The traditions, in their respect for individual freedom and the workings of God's grace in God's time, and their cautions against the dangers that power, money, and prestige hold for the unity of mission, might serve as a tool for the examination of institutional conscience.

I don't know whether any of this would work. Whatever might be done, however, I do know this. In the very starkness of its simplicity, unadorned by the creed, code, or cult of religion, A.A. offers an example of what I believe is the one thing necessary for a lifegiving spirituality. A.A. has found ways of supplying the missing link between *experience and faith*. Everything in A.A., I think now—the meetings, sponsorship, the steps, the telling of our stories, the fellowship, the anniversary celebrations, the literature—works to that end. And the observance of the traditions sees to it that nothing subverts the attaining of that end. Without that living link between experience and faith, that artery that goes to the heart of the believer, you have the dry bones of rules to be obeyed, dogmas to be believed, rituals to be performed, devoid of animating spirit.

Nora Gallagher, in *Things Seen and Unseen: A Year Lived in Faith,* puts it this way: "One imagines religion as making one 'good,' and various ideal ways of behaving are often touted in pulpits. But the opposite of sin is not virtue but faith. And none of it works without the weight of experience, knowing something as an experience rather than as an event that passes over the skin." That is what I have found in A.A., the link between the experience of being saved from my alcoholism by faith in a loving God and the truths and practices of the Catholic religious tradition. That is what I have been trying to say in this chapter. More, that may be what I have been trying to say in this whole book.

Several days before my anniversary celebration last January, the thought suddenly occurred to me: Hey, I'm an old-timer! I said to myself. I had seventeen years, more time in the program than happy, joyous, and free Tina had when I first came to A.A. in 1983. At the celebration I shared this thought and the wonderment and gratitude it brought me. Where had the time gone? It did not seem that long to me. As I looked back over the years of attending generally three meetings a week, I did not have the sense of dull and dreary repetition. A.A. had not grown "old" for me. I did not feel like someone who knew it all, who had nothing new to learn. Instead, with the memory of the misery of drinking still green for me, and a keen appreciation of all the blessings A.A. had brought me, I was looking forward to more. I see so much more clearly now the work that I still have to do on myself at deeper and deeper levels. There seems to be no end to it. But as the leader responded to me when I articulated that realization at a meeting some time later, "God asks more of us so that he can give us more." More freedom, more opportunities to carry the message, more love.

In the first week of April, another old-timer asked me to speak at a Saturday morning meeting that he chairs in a nearby town. Ted, now in his mid-thirties, was seventeen when I first met him; he had come into the program at fifteen. Several years ago he married a woman in A.A. Paula too was at the Saturday meeting, carrying her and Ted's baby in her arms. I had already had occasion to admire the baby at several noon meetings that Paula and I were attending. I was pleased to compliment Ted on his beautiful daughter.

Before the meeting began—there seemed to be mostly younger people in attendance—another young fellow came into the classroom, also carrying a baby. I recognized Tommy, the son of a former colleague of mine. I had put him in touch with one of our nuns who is a canon lawyer when he was seeking an annulment from his first marriage. I clucked over his lovely baby too. As the first speaker told his story, I could see Tommy in his baseball cap, his infant daughter holding onto his two index fingers, dancing in her little pink Doctor Dentons on the top of the desk.

I did not see Jennifer enter the classroom, but as I was speaking I noticed her, another thirty-something holding a baby. She and her brother used to come to my group when they were in their late teens. Her son has her electric platinum blond hair and her bright blue eyes. More clucking from me.

Driving home after the meeting, I found myself grateful for A.A. in a new way. Imagine the lives of those babies if their alcoholic parent or parents were still drinking. The erratic behavior, the emotional turmoil, the fights, the terror, the shame they would experience. Instead, even given the genetic factor in the disease of alcoholism, there is a good chance that the awful chain linking one alcoholic generation to another will be broken. These children will be raised by parents with all of the resources of Alcoholics Anonymous at their disposal, parents with a degree of emotional stability, responsible, who are committed to living a spiritual life, and who have the tools of the program and the support of the fellowship to help them deal with the inevitable disappointments and sorrows of life. I felt then not only like an old-timer but like a grandmother who has reason to look forward with hope to a better life for those who come after her.

And then, I thought again: What if Bill Wilson had turned to the bar instead of to the telephone booth in that hotel in Akron? "It's a God-given program," we say. I believe it. Thanks be to God for Alcoholics Anonymous.

Acknowledgments

By the time you have finished reading this book, you will understand, I trust, why Alcoholics Anonymous does not engage in public relations of any sort and counsels its members to maintain personal anonymity about membership in A.A. at the level of the media. In accord with the Eleventh and Twelfth Traditions, therefore, this book is published under the pen name of Sister Molly Monahan. By the same principles, the names of other A.A.s mentioned in the book have been changed, even though I have received their permission to publish what you have read here. I wish to thank them and other A.A. members for all that I have learned from them.

I fully subscribe to the traditions of anonymity. But maintaining my anonymity in a book about Alcoholics Anonymous does not preclude naming those who have been of such help to me in writing it. I think with great gratitude of James W. Lewis, Executive Director of The Louisville Institute, from which I received the grant that made it financially feasible for me to pursue this project.

And Suzanne Hoover, my writing mentor, who guided and encouraged me every step of the way with her astute advice and unfailingly generous support. The many comments, queries, suggestions, corrections, and cuts that Cindy Spiegel, my editor at Riverhead Books, penciled on the manuscript in two revisions gave me a new under-standing of the term "close reading" and a new apprecia-tion of the work of an editor who is dedicated to clarity, simplicity, and candor. It is simply true to say that without the help of these two women I would not have been able to write the book that you have in your hands. I am grateful also to Erin Bush, Cindy Spiegel's assistant, for her services, always graciously rendered.

Finally, I wish to thank my family, friends, and the members of my religious community whose interest and affection have sustained me from beginning to end.

Permissions

All scriptural quotations are taken from the New Revised Standard Version of the Bible, copyright 1989, Division of Christian Education of the National Council of the Churches of Christ in the United States of America.

Excerpts from the books *Alcoholics Anonymous, The Twelve Steps and Twelve Traditions,* and the short form of *Twelve Steps and Twelve Traditions* are reprinted with permission of Alcoholics Anonymous World Services, Inc. (A.A.W.S.). Permission to reprint these excerpts does not mean that